T0058777

The Book of Common Prayer: A Very Short Introduction

VERY SHORT INTRODUCTIONS are for anyone wanting a stimulating and accessible way into a new subject. They are written by experts, and have been translated into more than 45 different languages.

The series began in 1995, and now covers a wide variety of topics in every discipline. The VSI library currently contains over 550 volumes—a Very Short Introduction to everything from Psychology and Philosophy of Science to American History and Relativity—and continues to grow in every subject area.

Very Short Introductions available now:

Available soon:

For more information visit our website

www.oup.com/vsi/

Brian Cummings

THE BOOK OF COMMON PRAYER

A Very Short Introduction

OXFORD
UNIVERSITY PRESS

Great Clarendon Street, Oxford, OX2 6DP,
United Kingdom

Oxford University Press is a department of the University of Oxford.
It furthers the University's objective of excellence in research, scholarship,
and education by publishing worldwide. Oxford is a registered trade mark of
Oxford University Press in the UK and in certain other countries

© Brian Cummings 2018

The moral rights of the author have been asserted

First edition published in 2018

All rights reserved. No part of this publication may be reproduced, stored in
a retrieval system, or transmitted, in any form or by any means, without the
prior permission in writing of Oxford University Press, or as expressly permitted
by law, by licence or under terms agreed with the appropriate reprographics
rights organization. Enquiries concerning reproduction outside the scope of the
above should be sent to the Rights Department, Oxford University Press, at the
address above

You must not circulate this work in any other form
and you must impose this same condition on any acquirer

Published in the United States of America by Oxford University Press
198 Madison Avenue, New York, NY 10016, United States of America

British Library Cataloguing in Publication Data
Data available

Library of Congress Control Number: 2018941163

ISBN 978-0-19-880392-8

Printed and bound by CPI Group (UK) Ltd, Croydon, CR0 4YY

Contents

List of illustrations

Note on quotations

Quotations from the *Book of Common Prayer* are taken from the
Oxford World's Classics edition: *The Book of Common Prayer:
The Texts of 1549, 1559, and 1662*, ed. Brian Cummings (Oxford,
2013), using the abbreviation OWC. Citations from the 1549,
1559, and 1662 texts refer directly to that edition; quotations
from 1552 are also keyed to the 1559 text wherever it is identical.
Quotations from scripture unless otherwise noted refer to the King
James Bible; works by Shakespeare, to *The Oxford Shakespeare*.

Introduction: Understanding the *Book of Common Prayer*

The *Book of Common Prayer* is among the best-known books in human history. Apart from two brief interludes, it was the official book of Christian worship in England from 1549 to 2000. Even now that *Common Worship* (2000) has replaced it, its services continue to be used. The British Empire imposed its use on peoples all over the globe, so that it became translated into nearly 200 languages and dialects. Versions of 16th-century English can be heard to this day in Canada, in India and East Asia, all over Africa, and in Australasia and the Pacific islands. The book is not only a national monument but a post-colonial relic. In the USA, which celebrated the bicentenary of its independence more than a generation ago, it is still used every day. Up to a billion people have said prayers together, got married, or buried their families and friends, saying its words.

One way of understanding the *Book of Common Prayer* is thus as an example of liturgy. Liturgy is the term for a set form of words and gestures in a religious ritual. Liturgy is one of the oldest forms of Christian writing, some of its phrases pre-dating the formation of the New Testament. The most fundamental of early liturgies are Baptism and the Eucharist, based on the sayings and deeds of Jesus in the gospels. According to scripture, John the Baptist baptized Jesus in the River Jordan; and on his last night alive,

Jesus broke bread and took wine with his disciples, telling them to do so in future, 'in remembrance of him'. These came to be known as sacraments, actions that are sacred in their own right. Liturgies were also created for other occasions: for marriage, for burial, and the ordination of priests. Christian belief, then, has always been founded not only on the Bible, but on a set of *practices* which define the worship of God. The liturgy of St James of Jerusalem in the Orthodox church goes back to the 4th century CE; the liturgy of St Basil in the Coptic church to the 4th century; in the Western Catholic Church, a manuscript of the Leonine sacramentary survives from the 7th century, but its origins are much older. Like the Bible, liturgies were translated from language to language as Christianity spread. Differences in ritual practice, and in the meaning of sacrament, have been at the heart of Christian controversy and sectarian conflict ever since. The European Reformations, for example, fought over ritual as much as they did doctrine. Yet almost all Christian groups have retained some kind of rite, at least of Baptism and the Eucharist, and there is a core of similarity between all such practices.

However, while the *Book of Common Prayer* is a liturgy, it is also a carrier of national identity. The Church of England is a national church, which has been used to define the nation as a political entity. The British monarch to this day is the head of the Church, and is bound to it by oath. In turn, the Church of England has been tied in its nature to this book. While many people refer to the King James Version of the Bible as 'the authorized version', this is a misnomer invented in the 19th century. The 'authorized' book of the church of Edward VI was the *Book of Common Prayer*, which by the Act of Uniformity in 1549 was declared the *only* legal liturgy in England. Further Acts of Uniformity signed in 1559 and 1662 repeat this hegemony. The book is thus by definition not only religious but political. Loyalty to the nation was regulated for centuries by allegiance to the *Book of Common Prayer*, and political office was denied until the 19th century to anyone who refused to accept it.

The *Book of Common Prayer* contains prayers for the health of the monarch, by name, and for the success of her government. Politics and religion came together in this book, representing the first and last word on Christian practice in the English-speaking world. Articles of Religion, fifty-three in 1553, reduced to thirty-nine in 1560, fleshed out the theological implications of this practice, and after 1662 the Articles were commonly printed as an appendix to the *Book of Common Prayer*. The remarkable thing is that a book, written in haste for a boy king who reigned for only six years, came to preside over a worldwide empire, for centuries, embodying an ideal—and an ideology—of a religious nation.

Is the *Book of Common Prayer* at heart Catholic or Protestant? That is a very English question; the Very Short answer is 'Protestant'. The *Book of Common Prayer* came into being with the English Reformation, in order to declare the victory of Protestantism over the church of Rome. However, even though it replaced medieval rituals, the text created in 1549 directly translated many of those rituals from Latin into English. So, while the Catholic Queen Mary I abolished the *Book of Common Prayer* for being Protestant, a hundred years later, Puritans in Parliament successfully abolished it again for being too Catholic. Also, the peculiar polity chosen for the Church of England was that its head, the monarch, governed via bishops (an 'episcopacy'). That is, the church retained a hierarchy of bishops and archbishops, led by the Archbishop of Canterbury. The *Book of Common Prayer* is predicated on the authority of bishops, but is also the place where their authority is created, in the services for consecration of bishops, and ordination of priests and deacons. Archbishops consecrate bishops who in turn ordain priests and deacons. Originally a separate book called the *Ordinal* contained these services; after 1662, they became part of the single book.

Uniformity and hierarchy are central to the *Book of Common Prayer* from its beginning. To this, over time, was added a third rule: conformity. The book is an embodiment of what English social order looks like, even when practised on the other side of the world. Like many kinds of conformity, this could be voluntary as well as imposed. A liturgy is a book of everyday life, a place for worship of the divine, but also for the care of the self in the face of sickness, anxiety, and death. The *Book of Common Prayer* has inspired much love, not least as its end came into view. Over time, the language of the book has been held up by many, not only as a model of its kind, but as a jewel of English literary prose. Yet for others, whether in Roman Catholic and non-conformist Birmingham or Newcastle-upon-Tyne, or Ireland, India, or Australia, it has been a bastion of exclusion, oppression, and sometimes slavery.

This also leaves a problem for a *Very Short Introduction*. The *Book of Common Prayer*, more than most books, has divided users between those to whom it grants a sense of belonging, and those whom it excludes. My *Very Short Introduction* aims to be inclusive of all readers. Understanding the *Book of Common Prayer* requires many approaches: historical, linguistic, theological, ethical, political, literary. Like all liturgy, the *Book of Common Prayer* aspires to be universal, and to exist outside time. Yet more than perhaps any other book, this one embodies a particular people and a history.

Chapter 1
Ritual and the Reformation

Sometime in the reign of Elizabeth I, an account was written of the final years of the great cathedral priory at Durham, called the *Rites of Durham*. Surveying the ancient monuments of the monastic buildings before their dissolution in 1539, the text describes in detail its daily rituals. At the high altar stood statues in fine alabaster of the Virgin Mary and St Cuthbert, the patrons of the church. The sacrament was kept under a sumptuous canopy upon which perched a gilded silver pelican giving her blood to her young ones, 'in token that Christ did give his bloud for the sinns of the world'. When the monks went to sing the high Mass, putting on their vestments, they progressed with reverence to the high altar, bowing to the sacrament as they went:

> the gospeller did carrye a marvelous faire booke which had the Epistles and Gospells in it, & did lay it on the altar the which booke had on the outside of the coveringe the picture of our saviour Christ all of silver of goldsmiths worke...verye fine to behould, which booke did serve for the pax in the masse. The epistoler when he had sung the epistle did lay the booke againe on the altar and after when the gospell was sunge the gospeller did lay it downe on the altar, untill the masse was done.

The *Rites of Durham* could, without much exaggeration, be called the last rites of medieval England. Written (in one copy) on a parchment roll sixty-seven feet in length, it is a lament for the religion of the old days before the Reformation. Its central narrative is the desecration of the shrines of St Cuthbert and the Venerable Bede in the reign of Henry VIII. The author describes bones scattered, sculptures defaced, stained glass broken, and marble basins for holy water removed by the wife of the Protestant Dean, to be used in her kitchen. But the story also tells a lost way of life: how bishops and monks were buried, how poor children were taught, and aged women cared for in the almery. Threaded through this is a sense of mourning for the life (and books) of the liturgy. We imagine the feast of St Mark's Day; likewise Rogation days, when the Prior and the monks walked in solemn festival to St Oswald's in Elvet and St Margaret's in Framwellgate; or Whitsun, when sacred relics—a silver and gold image of St Oswald; the head of St Aidan; and the black 'rood' (cross) of St Margaret of Scotland—were displayed. Above all, the text remembers elaborate processions, such as for Corpus Christi, the Thursday after Trinity Sunday: beginning at Palace Green, then encircling the bailey of the castle, and heading finally through the city.

The author of the *Rites* is usually assumed to be a former monk of Durham. Recent scholarship suggests instead that he was neither a monk, nor even an eyewitness of what he appears to recall. The *Rites* is a polemic about Elizabethan Durham, and how the rites of the church are performed in this new world. The author wears his heart on his sleeve, and is clearly a staunch traditionalist. Some copies of the *Rites* were owned by 'recusant' Catholics, who refused the new rituals. However, the account is not a straightforward description of daily life in the Middle Ages. It is constructed memory, tugging at the hearts of its readers and persuading them of the folly of the Reformation.

My book tells the story of how a new religion replaced the old, with ritual and liturgical texts centre stage. These changes are not linear or simple, as in the Durham account. First, it may surprise us that while the monastery was suppressed in 1539, the Roman liturgy remained (if not quite intact) in the post-monastic cathedral and chapter. As late as 1547, Henry VIII was buried at Windsor with a Requiem Mass. His coffin even rested overnight at Syon Abbey, which he had closed eight years before. It was only in 1549 under his infant son, Edward VI, that an Act of Parliament banned the Latin Mass and introduced a vernacular form of ritual, the *Book of Common Prayer*. The ban lasted just four years, until Henry's daughter Mary I brought back Catholicism.

Other fabricated memories inform the *Rites*. William Whittingham (d.1579), the new Dean, is presented as a cardboard villain, but he was a learned man, a translator (while in exile in Frankfurt and Geneva under Mary) of the Geneva Bible. In 1563, under Elizabeth, one of his first acts was to establish regular services, using the now restored *Book of Common Prayer* (1559), with morning and afternoon sermons on Sunday. Another sermon on Wednesdays accompanied the fast which he introduced. Whittingham also encouraged music, purchasing new anthems by Thomas Tallis (*c*.1505–85) and other composers favoured in the Chapel Royal. Not least of the ironies of the *Rites of Durham* is that one of the manuscripts of this work was later owned by John Cosin (1595–1672). Cosin as a reviser of the *Book of Common Prayer* in 1662 revived medieval ritual practices that would have shocked Whittingham. In 1660 he became Bishop of Durham, rebuilding the choir stalls and an enormous Gothic font cover which reaches up to the vault to this day.

The medieval Mass

Masses were said every day in Durham Cathedral, although not always at the high altar: there were over twenty altars in all, nine in the choir alone. The daily ornaments were of red velvet, wrought with great flowers of gold in fine needlework embroidery known as *opus anglicanum*. For the principal feast of the Assumption of Our Lady, white damask beset with pearls and precious stones was used, 'which made the ornaments rich and gorgeous to behold'.

Sights like this, if less grand, were familiar in every parish in the country. Eamon Duffy comments: 'The liturgy lay at the heart of medieval religion, and the Mass lay at the heart of the liturgy.' Parish Mass was said or sung every Sunday, and on other holy days; by endowment, a 'votive' Mass on weekdays could be said. Lay devotion manifested itself especially at the feasts of saints. In late medieval England St Katherine protected against disease; St Brigid of Kildare aided the inner life; in the north, St John of Beverley and St William of York attracted regional loyalty.

The laity received Communion only once a year at Easter, having confessed their sins to the priest the week before. However, Mass on Sundays was an expectation for all, the apex of the rite being the elevation of the bread (the body of Christ) by the priest. Here, all five senses came into play. The sound of bells, the smell of incense, the sight of candles, the touching of hands, the taste of offerings, created a synaesthesia of devotion.

In the largest churches, several Masses were celebrated at the same time, staggered to allow a sermon to be heard at one, while viewing the elevation at another. Gentry heard Masses at different times the same day. Margaret Paston recalls her neighbour hearing three Masses one morning, coming home to his wife 'never the merrier'; he then went to the garden for further devotion before taking his dinner. Hearing Mass brought bodily benefits beyond succour for the soul: mothers in labour anticipated a safe delivery, a traveller a safe return home. 'Thy fote that day shall not thee fayll', a song went. Mass was never more pressing than at death. Margery Kempe describes the Corpus Christi guild in King's Lynn processing with the sacrament through the streets during pestilence to help the dying to a final resting place.

The Mass was thus a social rite and a public occasion. Richer families endowed private Masses in side-chapels or on weekdays, sometimes owning their own 'parclose' (a screened box), such as the Spring chantry at Lavenham in Suffolk. High Mass on Sundays combined sociability with worship. It was no contradiction that the priest spoke words in an ancient language or (at the most crucial moment) with his back to the congregation. The Mass was a complex service with different levels of participation. In the first part, up to the end of the offertory, when the bread and wine were placed at the altar, people might walk about, or just be coming in, chatting with neighbours. After the Confiteor (confession of sin), the banns of marriage were announced. A change of atmosphere came with the bidding of the bedes: vernacular prayers for the fruits of the earth, for nobles and magistrates, friends and enemies, and also for the dead.

Until the bell for *Sanctus*, only the devout might be in earnest prayer; for the most part, in John Bossy's words, 'the parish was being itself'. But the church fell quiet for the Canon that followed, called in German the *Stillmesse*. Once the elevation of the host took place, some would drift out to the inn; others remained throughout the Canon, the holiest of all parts of the ritual, in which the priest consumed the elements. There followed the ancient custom of the kiss of peace, either mouth to mouth, or increasingly, following an English invention, by using a transitional substitute called the pax, an image of Christ or of the cross which was passed from hand to hand and kissed by each in turn. Now Mass ended with a final blessing.

Devout or cynical, female or male, high or low, a typical parishioner knew enough to understand what was going on: the priest made satisfaction for the living and the dead, and in the eating of the bread a connection was inferred between a basic human function and the supernatural. John Mirk (fl.1380?), an Augustinian canon, and author of two guides for priests in the conduct of the Mass and other rituals, wrote in a sermon for Corpus Christi that the church offers the body of Christ every day at the altar 'In remission of synne to alle that lyven here in perfite charite and in great sokor and reles [succour and release] of her payne that ben in purgatori'. Bodily ritual at the same time brings together the social body of the community.

The Office of the Dead

Scarcely less familiar than the Mass was the liturgy for the dead, which combined many functions performed in different locations. Before death, at the visitation of the sick, a crucifix was held in front of the dying person in a final opportunity for penance. The viaticum, the last journey of the living human, led to confession. Communion was then received to complete 'extreme unction'. This was one of the seven sacraments, but as well as a theological action, the final hours of life were surrounded by informal rituals.

The Eucharist was brought to the sick in a procession with accompanying lights and incense. While the priest made his way to the deathbed, tolling of bells alerted the neighbourhood. Further rites after death provided for laying the body out; watching over it (the 'wake'); making and reading the will; carrying the body to church. All of this preceded the Office of the Dead: a Mass for the dead (a 'requiem') combined with other rites; a Vespers (or *placebo*); and a Matins and Lauds combined (called *dirige*). The fullest funeral rites involved the seven Penitential Psalms, and the Litany (a series of petitions).

Official liturgy accompanied extraordinary cultural phenomena such as the *danse macabre* ('dance of death') and the *ars moriendi* ('the art of dying'). In the former, visual representations of different estates—from pope, emperor, and knight, down to merchant, lawyer, and peasant—confront a grinning corpse. In the latter, prevalent in Germany in the 15th and early 16th centuries, an elaborate moral commentary surrounds the moment of death, promoting devotion, saintly living, and humility. This perhaps gives a morbid air, and accounts of medieval Christianity sometimes wallow in the grotesque. This underestimates what was a practical theory for living in the context of mortality, that recognized the significance of the departed in the lives of those left behind, and speculated on the possibility of an afterlife.

This, too, was a community affair, not only for kith and kin. Trade guilds enjoined members to attend the funeral of each of their brothers and sisters in work. Charitable giving was an expectation. Care for the dead continued after death: commemorative Masses were endowed at anniversaries. At the heart of this was the idea of 'purgatory': a third liminal world between hell and heaven, a vast waiting room for the majority of souls, neither saintly nor irredeemable, who paid their dues for sins in the expectation of eternity. To help them on their way, 'indulgences' (a grant of remission) could be purchased by their survivors, in a kind of spiritual mortgage. Saying Mass for the dead was a way for the living to maintain contact with the dead, to cherish them, and to provide an example for others to do the same when their turn came.

If purgatory seems abstract, it was given physical location by the graveyard outside the church. On the eve and feast of All Souls, the parish came together to pray for 'all the faithful departed', even those long-forgotten or unprovided for in wills. As well as a formal requiem and procession round the churchyard, this included ringing church bells through the night, lighting bonfires, or children placing cakes on graves. If in the privatized world of post-modern death it has become customary to shovel off relatives with minimum ceremony, or reduce Halloween to trashy kitsch and freakshows, it is salutary to be reminded of a world which could join hands across the boundary of death.

Ritual books and Books of Hours

St Justin Martyr describes a version of the Mass in his *Apology* of *c.*150 CE, consisting of a reading of an epistle and gospel, a sermon, an intercession, kiss of peace, offertory, thanksgiving, and communion. Three early textual types of sacramentary (a book for use by a priest during Mass) survive in the Latin West from the 7th century: Leonine, Gelasian, and Gregorian. Monastic orders developed liturgies from such forms, which varied throughout Europe, becoming known as the Roman rite of the later Middle Ages.

As liturgy became more elaborate, a larger range of books and texts came to be required. The most common (and complex) was the priest's Breviary (also known as *Portiforium*), a compendium of rites bringing together the parts of the divine office (Box 1), with variations for the liturgical seasons, each of which required a different set of psalms, prayers, hymns, and antiphons (and their music). Designed to be portable (hence its name) it was barely so, often divided into summer and winter volumes.

Although many breviaries contained the Canon and Ordinary of the Mass, this was insufficient to celebrate the Mass in full. The most sacred of the liturgical books was therefore the *Missale*. Beginning with a Calendar of holy days, a missal contained two large sections, the Temporal, with the annual cycle of Sundays

Box 1 The Canonical Hours

The 'divine office' (or Opus Dei) is divided into nine periods of prayer through the day and night, beginning with Matins (the first of the 'major hours', originally recited at midnight, including sung psalms, a long passage from scripture, and the hymn *Te Deum*); Lauds (the dawn office); Prime, Terce, Sext, and None (shorter daytime offices known as 'the little hours'); Vespers (the evening office and second 'major hour', with psalms, scripture, and *Magnificat*); and Compline (at going to bed). Monks and canons (clerics living in community under a rule) recited the whole Psalter each week divided between the Hours. Special readings and chant were set for saints' days.

starting at Advent; and the Sanctoral, with the fixed-day feasts
(aside from the Christmas period, which were in the Temporal),
mostly consisting of saints' days, starting with St Andrew on
30 November, which marked the beginning of the liturgical year,
looking forward to Christmas. At the heart of the book stood
the Canon and Ordinary of the Mass. This was often illuminated
in special ways, and even in printed copies was often on vellum
(parchment), because these pages wore out the quickest, and
because they contained the sacred mystery of the Eucharist.

Missals contained chant, but for a choir to sing the liturgy a
Gradual (book of chant) was also required. Larger churches
had an epistle book (Epistoller) and a gospel book (Gospeller),
organized not in biblical order but via the liturgical seasons.
A Processional was a collection of the chants and rites used in
processions on important festivals, such as the Rogation season
described in the Rites of Durham. These were supplemented
with books for special services: a Pontifical for bishops, containing
services like confirmation, ordination of priest and deacons,
dedications of churches, and even coronations. For a parish priest,
a Manual contained the rites of passage so critical to pastoral life:
baptism, marriage, visitation of the sick, and burial. Baptism
and marriage contained sections in the vernacular, for the laity
to be able to participate willingly. All these services were adapted
to local traditions (Box 2).

As the *Rites of Durham* vividly describes, ritual books were
not only practical texts but sacred objects in their own right.
They were vessels for sacred mysteries, embodying a transitional
status, as carriers of the holy. Like the Durham Gospel, such books
might be elaborately decorated with leather embossings, or gilt,
or hand-made silver pictures of Christ or a saint. Books were held
aloft in procession through the church and outside. Missals or
Bibles were carried around the neck in satchels, or cases of leather
or metal in the hand, protecting from damage but also granting
the object veneration.

Box 2 Uses

The Roman rite in principle extended throughout Western Europe, but was subject to local variation. Monasteries would use versions regulated by their individual orders. Parish churches in the southern and western regions of England, and in Wales and Ireland, increasingly preferred what was known as the Sarum Use: originally the liturgy of Salisbury Cathedral (before the new building was begun in 1220), it became much the most widespread rite in the province of Canterbury (which contained fourteen dioceses) from the 13th century onwards. In the north of England it was rivalled by the York Use (in its three dioceses). There were also at different times smaller Uses including Bangor, Exeter, Hereford, Lincoln, and London. Five of these are referred to in the preface to the *Book of Common Prayer*.

Texts inside the books included rites, prayers, hymns, and scripture (especially psalms, gospels, and epistles). They also contained instructions for sacred performance: rules of gesture, whether of devotion, genuflection, consecration, malediction, or benediction. In a missal these priestly actions acquired a quasi-sacred condition by being written or printed in red (hence 'rubric'). The lectern was bathed in incense at the reading of the gospel, the book borne in procession and kissed by the priest before and after. At the offertory of the paten and cup for Communion, each object was raised, then crossed, then covered in incense several times, the priest kissing his hand. At the beginning of the Canon, the priest looked with veneration on the host; he lifted himself up, joined his hands, wiped his fingers, bowed to the host, and afterwards raised it above his forehead, that it might be visible to all. He repeated this process with the wine, elevating the chalice as high as the breast, or else above the head, and afterwards raised his arms in the form of a cross, the fingers being joined. Gesture as much as word was therefore involved in the invocation of holiness that took place in the Mass.

These rituals of the everyday performed what has been called a 'social miracle'. Medieval liturgy joined together different parts of the community, and staged its rites of passage, from birth through adolescence into sexual maturity, up to burial in the ground. This was a public religion, but participation in the ritual year also took place privately through Books of Hours ('primers'). These are the popular books of the Middle Ages. Early examples (from the 13th century) were the preserve of the wealthy, and richly decorated. But by the 15th century cheaper versions became available, and in the early 1500s an unbound printed primer could be bought for 3d or 4d.

The contents of a Book of Hours were in Latin, consisting of variable elements which usually included: the Little Hours of the Virgin, for daily recitation; and the Office of the Dead in two parts (known, from their initial words, as *placebo* and *dirige*). The latter provided not only a practical guide during mourning, but also a *memento mori* (a reminder of death). To these were added the seven Penitential Psalms; the fifteen 'gradual' psalms; and often prayers in honour of the holy cross, the Five Wounds of Christ, or the 'Fifteen Oes' of St Bridget of Sweden. Many primers were made for women. Illuminations, of initials or whole pages (sometimes tipped in at a separate stage of production), provided markers in using the book, or stimulated devotion. Books of Hours indicate increasing literacy, but reading was not their only purpose. They were aids to devotion; a mnemonic for the recitation of prayers known by heart; and also objects of devotion, to be carried on the person, to be touched or raised during veneration or meditation.

The challenge to tradition

When Martin Luther (1483–1546) wrote his 'Ninety-Five Theses' in 1517, he was not immediately attacking the ritual life of the medieval church. The formal object of his campaign was indulgences (the sale of remission in purgatory). Yet in declaring that indulgences were futile, and that the whole life of a Christian should be one of penitence, he was already encroaching on the sacramental system of penance: 'No one is sure that his own contrition is sincere; much less that he has attained full remission' (Thesis 30). By subverting the practice of giving pardons for specific acts, he also cast doubt on the idea of purgatory, if not yet questioning the doctrine.

Luther's Reformation has been called 'an accidental revolution'. His theological creativity took on a momentum of its own, drawing him into broader conflicts, until little was left untouched. He also drew on cultural movements that were not so much doctrinal as anthropological. Erasmus (*c*.1466–1536) developed a practical theology for the new age in the *Enchiridion militis christiani* ('Handbook of a Christian Knight') first written in 1501, then a bestseller in a revised edition of 1518. His argument based itself on a dialectical contrast between spirit and flesh, derived from Origen and other studies in neo-Platonism. This took him into the muddy waters of ritual, and the material representation of the sacred.

Of baptism, he says: 'What is the use of being sprinkled with a few drops of holy water as long as you do not wipe clean the inner defilement of the soul?' On the cult of the saints, the veneration of relics, and the making of images, he says similarly there is little point in worshipping the bones of St Paul or a statue of the Virgin, if we are ignorant of her virtuous life, or the wisdom of his writing. From here, Erasmus is a step away from the Eucharist, on which subject he is respectfully evasive, advocating that bread and wine be consumed 'spiritually'. The truest image of Christ, Erasmus says, comes in scripture. The preface to his 1516 Greek New Testament (the first in print) says Christ is figured better in scripture than in his bodily life.

By 1523 Luther's Reformation in Wittenberg attacked the sacrifice of the Mass. It made no sense, he said, for Christ's sacrifice to be repeated every week. Christ redeemed mankind in a single action forever on the cross. Private Masses were sinful, especially requiem Masses. His first liturgy (the *Formula*) was conservative: he retained the Latin language, vestments, and the elevation of the host. But the Canon was savaged, and Communion was to be consumed by the laity on all occasions, in both kinds.

If this wasn't radical enough, in 1525 Huldrych Zwingli (1484–1531) persuaded the Zürich Council to cancel Mass, and introduce a Communion liturgy in the German language. Unlike Luther, Zwingli denied the real presence, making Mass a celebration of remembrance, rather than a divine action. This was accompanied by physical changes to ritual. Wooden cups and plates avoided outward displays of formality. The congregation sat at tables to emphasize that the sacrament was a meal. The sermon formed the focal point of worship, and there was no organ music or singing.

The English Reformation began as a political revolution, with Henry VIII's marriage to Anne Boleyn in 1533, and the Act of Supremacy in November 1534. This made Henry head of the church. Reformers quickly took advantage of a change in religious regime, by attacking purgatory and the cult of saints. William Marshall (d.1540) produced a primer in English which omitted the saints in the Litany and *dirige*. Traditional religion took a further battering with the trial and execution of Thomas More (1478–1535). More had acted as Catholic England's bastion for a decade, leading a campaign against Luther.

Protestants presented the Mass as a barrier to the common man, urgently demanding a vernacular service, with Communion administered regularly to the faithful, in both kinds. Surviving Mass books suggest a different story, with traditional religion thriving in the life of communities before, during, and after the Reformation. Lambeth Palace Library MS 5066 is a York Use Missal dating to the 15th century. Handwritten additions itemize gifts for use in the church of All Hallows, Broughton, Lancashire in 1512. These provide a new chalice (the cup for the wine), a vestment and surplice (clothing for the priest), a Mass-book, a lamp for the rood (the cross at the entrance to the choir of the church), a pyx (container for the host), two paxes, and a *sanctus* or 'sacring' bell (which signalled the elevation of the host). A Sarum Use missal (Cambridge University Library MS Add. 6688) declares on an end-paper that it is the gift in 1521 of William More (Prior of Worcester Cathedral), to the church of St John the Baptist in Bromsgrove.

Within two decades, however, this book bears the marks of Reformation. In the summer of 1535, to comply with the instructions of Thomas Cromwell (d.1540), the word *pape* (Pope) has been scrubbed out next to the names of St Clement, St Linus, and others in the Calendar. In the Canon of the Mass, the word *pape* is replaced with *rege* ('king') to show the new supreme authority of the king. Later, in 1538, the Mass for St Thomas Becket has been obliterated with red dye. It may be that Hugh Latimer (*c.*1485–1555), Bishop of Worcester, insisted on punctilious observation of royal edicts. Latimer preached a sermon on 9 June 1536 at the opening of the Convocation of the new English church, denouncing images ('clad in silk garments' and lighted with candles at midday), and dismissing relics (as 'pigs' bones'). The Ten Articles, declared at Convocation, reduced the seven sacraments to three—Baptism, Penance, and Eucharist.

Popular reaction to change was often negative. In Beverley in Yorkshire in October 1536, the parish priest failed to announce St Wilfrid's Day in the bidding of the bedes. After Mass, the whole parish was said to be in distress, even though the king's authority was proclaimed in justification. Beverley joined the Pilgrimage of Grace, a northern rebellion which defended the old practices well into the new year. At Horncastle in Lincolnshire, rebels designed a banner showing the Five Wounds of Christ and a chalice with the host.

In another arm of the new religious government, Cromwell initiated the process of examining religious houses, beginning with the smaller ones. Visitations in 1536 identified for immediate surrender any house with an annual net income under £200. If official policy at first was reform, moving monks and nuns to larger monasteries, in 1538 full-scale suppression was proposed, lands and revenues reverting to the king.

Alongside wholesale changes in religious and social organization, the dissolution ended recitation of the monastic office. Durham's routine of prayer from dawn to dead of night fell silent. Yet not all was lost. Over a hundred former monastic churches survived for parochial worship, in addition to fourteen former monastic churches that became cathedrals. In around a dozen cases, wealthy benefactors or parishes purchased a complete former monastic church from the commissioners, presenting it to their community as a parish church. Other parishes bought disused monastic woodwork, choir stalls, or stained glass windows. Many thought the old life would come back soon. Meanwhile Protestants saw the back side of the monks as a welcome sign of the coming apocalypse.

English ritual reformed

Old abbey churches, recycled for parish use, their other monastic buildings now walled off and derelict, stand as a symbol of the religious regime that prevailed, for the time being, in England. It is difficult now to respond to this dispassionately: nostalgia for the past competes with a narrative of modernity. This reflects deep anxieties and uncertainties at the time.

Government policy went this way and that, now enforcing Reformation, now retreating. Outspoken evangelical bishops, such as Latimer, and Nicholas Shaxton (c.1485–1556) of Norwich, resigned. Ritual life was reduced, yet in many respects continued as before. Parishes endowed with chantries, where a priest prayed for the souls of donors, continued unaffected. Surviving medieval ritual books symbolize these mixed fortunes of Reformation. York Minster Library MS XVI.I.3, a York Use Missal, has the word *pape* marked up for censorship with small crosses, but the work was never done. In other cases, books are left untouched by government orders, whether in defiance, or through idleness, or waiting for the tide to turn again.

Many books show the vicissitudes of changing politics. A printed Sarum missal surviving in Trinity College, Cambridge (shelf mark *C*.6.8) shows censorship under Henry VIII restored under Mary I after 1553, offensive words written back in as carefully as they were removed. On the flyleaf of a Sarum missal printed in 1510 (Lambeth Palace Library H2015.52.01) a new prayer is pasted in, 'to be sayd in the Masse for the Quenes highnesse, beinge with childe', although the child was a fantasy.

After 1555, new primers and missals were printed. One example (Cambridge University Library Rit.a.155.1) bears a handwritten addition asking for the reader to pray for the soul of Richard Perkins who has donated the book for the use of the church in Tempsford in Bedfordshire, dated 1557. At this point it must have seemed as if the old religion was back forever. But another hand has added at the top of the title page, showing history taking another turn: 'This booke I bought, to see ye errors of it, y^t I might ye better confute them.'

In January 1549 an Act of Parliament announced a new book of services. Henry VIII had been buried according to the old rites and his son Edward VI was on the throne. The new book was in English and came into force at Whitsun, although some copies were in use at the beginning of Lent. The story of the *Book of Common Prayer* will be told in Chapter 2. Yet as well as making a new book, the Act declared the end of the old one. The parish procession, the elevation of the host, the pax, were removed at one blow. Mass books, breviaries, manuals, graduals, whether of Sarum, York, or Hereford Use, were banned and destroyed. Not everyone complied, as is shown by the survival of copies under Mary. But while 8,000 missals were in use in England in 1500, one for every parish (in fact many more, since large churches and cathedrals possessed several), only about 200 survive today. Of the York Use, there are only twelve complete manuscript copies extant, plus twenty odd printed in the five 16th-century editions.

One copy may suffice as an emblem for the rest (Figure 1). It was printed in Rouen in 1516 for sale in York. In the 500 years of its life, it has not passed outside a small corner of North Yorkshire. An obit (record of the day of death) in the Calendar suggests its

1. York Missal, showing damage to a hand-painted woodcut of the crucifixion in the Canon of the Mass: *Missale ad vsum celeberrime ecclesie Eboracensis* (Rouen: P. Olivier, 1516). York Minster Library, shelf mark: Stainton 12 (Stainton Collection).

use by John Best, rector of Faceby in the North York Moors, up to 1530. In the 17th century it passed into the hands of a vicar of Stainton, a few miles to the north, becoming part of the parochial library there.

If you open the book at the Canon of the Mass you are confronted with an astonishing sight. There are two hand-painted woodcut illuminations, one of the crucifixion with the Virgin and St John the Evangelist; the other of God the father enthroned, surrounded by evangelists. Both images traditionally prefaced the *Te igitur*, the prayer which begins the most sacred part of the Roman rite. Across the crucifixion there is a slash right across the page, slicing the cross, though not quite touching the body of Christ. Underneath, you can see another, deeper gouge of a knife, crosswise, as if in a saltire. There is matching damage on the other side, through the other image. The knife has gone deep into the book, more than a dozen pages on each side. Perhaps mistaking God the father for the Pope (he wears a papal tiara, following conventional iconography)—or perhaps through a more primitive form of iconoclasm—God's face is split open by two smaller marks of the knife.

York Minster Library Stainton 12 is a wounded missal: it bears seven wounds in all, like the wounds of Christ. There is no other surviving ritual book of the English Middle Ages quite like it, painful evidence of the deep feelings on both sides, as the Reformation tore up a millennium of sacred worship and brought new forms of life into being.

Chapter 2
The making of the
Book of Common Prayer

The author of the *Book of Common Prayer* in 1549 was Thomas Cranmer, Archbishop of Canterbury (1489–1556). This is true in two senses: he authorized its passage through Parliament and into law, and he was also the prime 'author' in its formulation. However, authorship in the modern sense is not the proper term. The making of a vernacular prayer book comprised compilation of existing material rather than new composition. Indeed, its structure and sources are as complex as the English Reformation itself.

Cranmer and the English Reformation

Cranmer was born in Nottinghamshire and his early life, social and religious, was conventional: his sister was a Cistercian nun in Lincolnshire. Despite later attempts to align him with nascent Lutheranism at his university in Cambridge, Cranmer's passage towards a doctorate in theology and the priesthood appears to have been comfortably orthodox, perhaps conciliarist in emphasis. What changed his life as well as the religion of his country was the king's efforts to divorce Catherine of Aragon. In 1527, Cardinal Wolsey (1470–1530) hired him as one of twelve theological experts in 'the great matter'. Cranmer came to the king's personal attention in 1529, just as Wolsey fell from grace, unable to negotiate a settlement. Cranmer went to work on new arguments, including in 1531 his first efforts in writing at length in the English language. His skills included meticulous linguistic nuance and diplomacy, and in 1532 he became the king's new ambassador to the Holy Roman Emperor. This took him to Nürnberg, seat of the emperor's parliament, and the first of the imperial free cities to adopt Lutheranism.

Cranmer by this time was appropriating continental Reformed ideas for the king's benefit; among his contacts was Martin Bucer (1491–1551) of Straßburg. Of all the Reformed theologians, Bucer became the most consistent champion of the English cause, and a lifelong correspondent of Cranmer. He was of more immediate use than Luther, who took as dim a view of Henry's divorce as of his politics in general. Nürnberg was a key staging post in Cranmer's development. It was here that he first encountered Lutheran theology directly; here he experienced Reformed liturgy in the German vernacular; and here he married Margarete (d.1575), niece of the Nürnberg pastor Andreas Osiander (1498–1552). No sooner had Cranmer married, however, than he hid his wife away. For meanwhile, in October 1532, when Archbishop William Warham died, Cranmer was recalled from embassy to the vacant see at Canterbury. No priest, never mind bishop, could openly take a wife in the pre-Reformation church.

If Luther was an accidental revolutionary, Cranmer was a reactionary one. His career is full of turnarounds and even backsliding. His allies accused him of betrayal, and his enemies of hypocrisy. Yet without his fastidious and relentless pertinacity, the English Reformation is unimaginable. What propelled a man of such caution to enact such profound cultural change? He owed his preferment to the new queen, Anne Boleyn, who favoured the evangelical cause. Cranmer himself began to acquire humanist clients with Reformed leanings.

Perhaps the first doctrine on which Cranmer changed his mind was justification, the idea that first inspired Luther's new ideology.

Cranmer's annotations in the margin of his copy of Erasmus's *De libero arbitrio* ('On Free Will'), published against Luther in 1524, show him as an Erasmian; but over the next dozen years, leading to the Ten Articles in 1536 (in which Cranmer's handwriting is visible in draft), he moved to a position in which the only sufficient cause of salvation is God's mercy and grace. Works have no part in justification. However, he favoured Philipp Melanchthon (1497–1560) in his nuanced expressions on a need for works *after* justification, and for a corresponding emphasis on Christian exhortation to a moral life.

Melanchthon was the author of the Augsburg Confession of 1530, the first formal summary of Protestant beliefs, and also of the theological handbook *Loci communes* ('Common Places'), a new edition of which was dedicated to Henry VIII in 1535. Melanchthon provided a religious model that was independent of Rome, but respected a wise ruler: the two guiding lights in Cranmer's policy. However, Cranmer also carefully protected himself from exposure. He allowed Cromwell to dictate the pace of Reformation, and to initiate major interventions such as the dissolution of the monasteries. Cranmer even-handedly allowed the execution, for heresy, of John Frith, for denying the real presence in the Eucharist; and of Elizabeth Barton for 'prophesying', employing a potent cocktail of devotion to the Virgin Mary and attacks on Queen Anne.

The year 1536 saw full-scale rebellion in the Pilgrimage of Grace (see Chapter 1). In a letter to the Zürich theologian Heinrich Bullinger (1504–75), Cranmer expressed his consternation. But in another letter he showed concern at innovations in the theology of the Eucharist. Cranmer later in his life asserted that he occupied three doctrinal views on this subject at different times. In the 1520s he respected transubstantiation, the physical change in the elements first fully asserted in 1215 at the Lateran Council. In the late 1530s he followed something like a Lutheran position, rejecting the sacrifice of the Mass but allowing real presence. By the late 1540s he had abandoned this in favour of newer Swiss positions. Such careful deliberations show the emerging splits in Reformed confessions, sometimes around tiny points of dispute.

A liturgy in English

Policy on religion wavered back and forth as the king remarried and different factions fought for his attention. The Ten Articles of 1536 favoured the Protestants, influenced by the Wittenberg Articles; while the Six Articles of 1539 went the opposite way, reaffirming transubstantiation, auricular confession, and monastic vows. The Bishops' Book of 1537 similarly gave way to the more conservative King's Book of 1543. It is against this landscape that evangelicals began to experiment with vernacular forms of language in Reformed versions of English primers.

In 1530 George Joye (d.1553), who had worked with William Tyndale (d.1536) on the translation of the English Bible (not always with Tyndale's approval), produced a pioneering English primer printed by Martin de Keyser in Antwerp. Among its features was the adoption of the numbering of the Ten Commandments favoured in Zwinglian Zürich, emphasizing the prohibition on 'graven images'. While this gave impetus to the attack on images, Joye elsewhere showed caution. He included a Calendar, but made admonitory Protestant notes rejecting relics. While including an English version of the *Ave Maria* ('Hail Mary'), he deleted the *Salve Regina* ('Hail holy queen').

Other elements fluidly render the pre-Reformation primer in the vernacular: the *Magnificat* borrows from Tyndale's *New Testament*; the Lord's Prayer includes the experimental phrase 'Geve us this daye owre sufficiente fode', not found in any other version. The book is a hotchpotch: it proclaims its own biblicism, yet also includes the hymns *Te Deum* and *Benedicite*, from neither the Old nor the New Testament. Among its innovations are scriptural 'lessons' injected into Matins. But the feature of the book of which Thomas More complained was that it included neither Litany nor *dirige*.

More banned an English primer in the summer of 1530, and Bishop Stokesley banned Joye's *Ortulus anime* ('Little Garden of the Soul') in December 1531; it survives in one copy in the British Library. Yet in 1534 Marshall, one of Cromwell's agents in the monasteries, was permitted to produce a Reformed primer in English in London: this reprinted three-fifths of Joye's work, filling up the rest with unacknowledged translations from works by Luther such as the *Betbüchlein* ('Little Prayer Book'). Like the *Ortulus*, Marshall's book excluded the offices of the dead. In 1535, he produced a new *Goodly Primer*, again printed by John Byddell. Its preface denounced the *Salve Regina* and the Fifteen Oes. But it included the Litany and *dirige*. The book shows a competition between Reformed and traditional primers in Henry's new England. 1535 also sees a primer in English in the Sarum use, printed by Robert Redman.

In books like this we see the first traces of what was to become the *Book of Common Prayer*. Matins opens in Joye's *Ortulus*: 'O Lorde opene thow my lippes: then shal my mouthe shew forthe thy prayse'. In the Matins of 1549 this becomes: 'O Lorde opene thou my lippes', followed by the response, 'And my mouthe shall shewe forth thy prayse' (OWC, 7). In 1538, revising the text of the Bishops' Book in his own handwriting, Cranmer translated into English the Apostles' Creed, in a version repeated almost word for word in 1549. In 1538 there are also the first signs of Cranmer himself advancing the cause of a Reformed liturgy, with some parts in English. This was for the benefit of a Lutheran delegation from Germany arriving in London to pave the way for Henry's marriage to Anne of Cleves. It complained of continued 'abuses', such as withholding the cup from the laity during the Eucharist, and saying private Masses for the dead.

In manuscript, Cranmer planned a revised version of the Breviary, making use of the new Breviary produced by Cardinal Francisco de Quiñones (d.1540) for Pope Paul III. This perhaps seems an odd source, but it had the advantage of straightaway reducing the number of hours in the divine office from eight to two: Morning and Evening Prayer. Cranmer also made use of an order of service composed by Johannes Bugenhagen for Christian III of Denmark, who had just won a civil war to impose Lutheranism there. In his proposed new order Cranmer provided for everything that was needed in one book: including a Calendar heavily reducing the numbers of saints, with biblical figures making up the difference; a set of readings enabling the whole Bible to be heard through the year; and a sequence of psalms to be completed each month. Cranmer's draft was in Latin, but this may have been to enable the German delegation to follow it. There are suggestions Cranmer intended some (possibly all) of the office to be in English. Bible passages are supplied in English, in the Great Bible version proposed by Cromwell.

Nevertheless, even at enthusiastic moments of reform, no Henrician government came anywhere near promoting a new liturgy, never mind an English one. In 1542 Convocation reimposed the Sarum Breviary on the southern province. However, 'the names and memories of all saints, which be not mentioned in the scripture, or authentical doctors', are removed. Every Sunday and holy day, after the *Te Deum* and the *Magnificat*, a chapter of the New Testament is to be read aloud without further exposition; when the New was finished, the Old should begin.

The only exception to this liturgical status quo was in 1544, when an English Litany was published. Maybe prayers for the welfare of the king made such a book especially consonant with the religion of Henry VIII. It was followed in 1545 by the King's Primer, the first official primer of the regime. The king took a personal interest in the book. A notable feature is that the Lord's Prayer (Box 3), which existed in many different English forms, appears for the first time in the wording adopted in the *Book of Common Prayer* and used for centuries to come.

Box 3 The Lord's Prayer (or Paternoster) of 1545 and 1549

Oure father whiche arte in heaven, hallowed be thy name. Thy kyngdom come. Thy wyll be done in earth as it is in heaven. Geve us this daye oure dayly bread. And forgeve us oure trespasses, as we forgeve them that trespasse agaynst us. And leade us not into temptacion. But deliver us from evell. Amen. (OWC, 7)

Lurking behind these official procedures and proclamations lay a more visceral anxiety about the status of prayer. On the one hand, Protestants cast doubt on much of the liturgical inheritance of the Middle Ages as 'superstition' or abuse. On the other hand, Catholics cast doubt on the validity of prayers in English, or without the correct ritual actions accompanying them. A controversy that roared into life in Kent late in the reign shows evidence on both sides.

Known as the 'Prebendaries' Plot', this began as a move by conservatives to amass evidence that Cranmer was allowing heresy, and thus burn him at the stake. When Henry performed a U-turn and decided to punish both sides, Cranmer conducted a counter-examination and took the opportunity to carry out a purge of Mass-priests in the opposite direction. The evidence survives in Cambridge, Corpus Christi College MS 127, often in Cranmer's hand, or with his marginal annotations fulminating against depositions as 'Seditious' or 'error' or 'Images'.

In one direction, lamp tapers are taken away from in front of the sacrament, or the arms and legs of the rood are violently broken. On 25 July 1543, Margaret Toftes declares 'that her daughter could piss as good holy water as the priest could make any'. She has not crept to the cross for three years. It cannot be read in scripture that Our Lady is in heaven. Images are just devils and idols. Nicolas Fitzwilliams on 5 August 'maintained that prayers did not help souls departed'. In September, Robert Strawghwyn says that 'Saints could neither help nor hear us'. In these evangelical statements Latin prayers are ineffectual because the laity cannot understand them, and become mere 'mumbling'. However, in the other direction, such statements are taken as the railings of blasphemers.

Reparation is sought against Protestant damage in churches. In the parish of Milton, John Cross the cellarer, after the image of St Margaret is taken down, 'came to the same church and did set the same image again with a garland of flowers on the head of it, and did strowe [strew] the church and said mass there'. Far from Latin being a sign of the ineffectuality of prayer, it guarantees sacred performance. The parson of Ripley likens the 'paternoster' in English to the hard shell of a nut, the Latin version to its sweet kernel. Edward Dyngelden of Rolwynden 'obstinately refuses to learn his Paternoster, Ave, Creed and Ten Commandments in English'. To those who say prayer is impossible in an unknown tongue it is rebuffed that St Paul says *Nescit homo quomodo orandum sit, sed spiritus hominis docet quomodo orandum sit*—no one knows what he prays without the Holy Spirit speaking to him.

The second Reformation of Edward VI

On 28 January 1547, Edward VI, a boy of nine, followed his tumultuous father to the throne of England. Henry veered violently between identifying himself as political reformer and pious son of the old church. Despite favouring the latter tendency in his last years, at his death a conservative faction at court was falling. Thus Edward Seymour (d.1552) became Lord Protector to the boy king, soon ascending to be Duke of Somerset. Allied with powerful voices on the Privy Council (such as John Dudley and Cranmer himself), preferment rested on evangelical churchmen. Thus began England's 'Second

Reformation', putting into action a religious campaign both more experimental and more destructive than anything before.

Cranmer's homily at the coronation called Edward a new Josiah (the infant ruler in the Old Testament Book of Kings), urging him to see 'God truly worshipped, idolatry destroyed, and the tyranny of the bishops of Rome banished'. The first summer of the reign saw new Injunctions reinforced by visitations: an assault on traditional religion was extended, forbidding the burning of lights anywhere except on the altar before the sacrament. Destruction of images now included stained glass windows; processions were abolished; and Matins and Evensong were shortened to allow a chapter of the Bible to be read aloud in English.

These orders are a premonition of a wholesale vernacular liturgy, long the aspiration of evangelicals, but stalled or denied before. Some portions of English service were introduced in the Chapel Royal almost immediately. Parliament met in November and its first Act was to 'restore' Communion in both kinds while also abolishing compulsory confession before reception. Momentum gathered through the unexpected consequences of European politics. After victory at Mühlberg in the Schmalkaldic Wars, Charles V introduced Interim orders restricting Protestant worship. Thus in December 1547, the Italian reformers Peter Martyr Vermigli (1499–1562) and Bernardino Ochino (d.1564/5) arrived in England and lodged at Lambeth, along with Immanuel Tremellius (1510–80) the converted Jew and biblical scholar. Here Jan Łaski (1499–1560), the Polish Reformer, joined them, soon followed by the biggest name of all, Bucer, who became Regius Professor of Divinity at Cambridge while Vermigli mirrored his position at Oxford. If Cranmer had had his way Melanchthon himself might have been an English migrant.

In this zealous atmosphere, the godly dreamed of overcoming what they took to be widespread apathy towards reform, and devotion to the old ways. The first step was a new form of liturgy called *The Order of the Communion*, which was brought into use on Easter Day, 1548, and printed in time for the Frankfurt Book Fair. Strictly it covered only the distribution of the Communion among the laity, with the rest of the service in Latin following the old rite: but the exhortation, 'Dearly beloved in the Lord'; the confession and absolution; the 'comfortable words'; and 'prayer of humble access' all passed verbatim later into the *Book of Common Prayer*. Nonetheless, most of the new material was translated from sections in Sarum, although use was also made of Hermann von Wied's *Pia deliberatio* ('Pious Consultation'). This was a Latin translation of a German church order proposed (unsuccessfully) for Cologne in 1543, largely written by Bucer.

In December 1548 the House of Lords met to discuss the Eucharist in detail, a decidedly unusual event then as now. It was a useful venue in that it allowed all the available bishops to discuss the issue, while testing the waters among the secular powers, in a context where royal supremacy prevailed. Unlike for any of the drafting of the *Book of Common Prayer*, a manuscript survives in the British Library showing the highly controversial arguments in action. Cranmer's interventions, it has been demonstrated, show that he had by now moved to a third phase in his doctrinal opinion on the sacrament, more in line with the Swiss and less with the Lutherans. His insistence that the Eucharist is endowed only with the 'spiritual' presence of Christ, and that membership of the body of Christ is not dependent on the sacrament, drew an angry reaction from Thomas Thirlby (d.1570), Bishop of Westminster. The evangelicals prevailed, and on 19 December, the Commons began proceedings for a bill. After Christmas, the Act of Uniformity was passed, enforcing the new book as sole instrument of liturgy in England, banishing Sarum, York, and the rest into non-existence.

Cranmer's Register shows he was assisted in drafting the new book by bishops such as Thirlby, Thomas Goodrich (1494–1554) of Ely, Henry Holbeach (d.1551) of Lincoln, Nicholas Ridley (d.1555) of Rochester; and also William May (d.1560) the Dean of St Paul's, and Simon Haynes (d.1552), Dean of Exeter. However, the timescale ensured substantial reuse of material, such as royal primers, the *Litany* (1544), and the *Order of Communion* (1548). In terms of sources, the irony of the book is that it translated much of Sarum while at the same time supplanting it. Matins and Evensong abbreviated the Breviary; Communion a missal; Baptism, Marriage, and Burial, a Manual.

Yet even in borrowing from Sarum, much was changed. The book (Box 4) begins with the canonical hours, but cuts them down to just two: Morning and Evening Prayer. The Calendar was retained, to consternation among continental theologians. However, a distinction was made between 'red letter' saints—from scripture,

Box 4 Contents of the 1549 Book of Common Prayer

   i. A Preface.

  ii. A table and Kalendar for Psalmes and Lessons.

 iii. The ordre for Matins and Evensong, throughout the yeare.

 iv. The Introits, Collectes, Epistles and Gospelles, to be used at the celebracion of the lordes Supper, and holy Communion.

  v. The Supper of the Lorde and holy Communion, commonly called the Masse.

 vi. Of Baptisme, bothe publique and private.

 vii. Of Confirmacion, where also is a Cathechisme for children.

viii. Of Matrimony.

 ix. Of visitacion of the sicke, and Communion of the same.

  x. Of Buriall.

 xi. The purification of women.

 xii. Ashwednesdaie.

xiii. Of Ceremonies ommitted or reteyned.

xiv. Certein notes for the more plain explicacion and decent ministracion of thinges conteined in this boke.

given Collects and readings of their own—and the rest left in black, with no services.

The new Calendar drastically cut back the liturgical year, with no room for some of the greatest feasts of the Virgin, such as the Assumption, still less for popular late medieval cults such as St Anne. The Calendar left out celebrations of doctrine such as Corpus Christi and Holy Cross ('Holyrood'), although many are mentioned as worthy of private observation. Confusion over the cult of the saints increased when some returned to the book under Elizabeth, such as St George and St Edmund King and Martyr. The lingering attraction of these saints, along with St Swithun and St Crispin, perhaps shows the emergence of a cult of national virtues.

Elsewhere, confusion is doctrinal. The Eucharist is still called 'mass' in the title page (along with 'lord's supper', and 'communion'), though the word is removed elsewhere. This service is shot through with highly technical compromises. The word 'oblation' appears even though the doctrine of sacrifice is suppressed. An elaborate procedure for consecration is included, at one point even including the vexed word 'Canon'. Printed crosses denote manual actions at the moment of consecration:

> Heare us (o merciful father) we besech thee: and with thy holy spirite and worde, vouchsafe to bl✠esse and sanc✠tifie these thy gyftes, and creatures of bread and wyne, that they maie be unto us the bodye and bloude of thy moste derely beloved sonne Jesus Christe. (OWC, 30)

The Sarum rite at this point compares the offering of the elements of the Mass with the sacrifice offered by Christ on the cross. Cranmer makes do with a piece of punctuation, a silent colon. As a result, on the crucial topic of the real presence, the text is scrupulously opaque. Neither traditionalist nor reformer is truly satisfied, although Cranmer perhaps hoped that in compromise, reconciliation could be found.

The Communion

commaund vs to celebrate a perpetuall memorye of that his precious death, vntyll his comming again: Heare vs (O merciful father) we beseech thee: and with thy holy spirite and worde vouchsafe to bl+esse and sanc+tifie these thy gyftes, and creatures of bread and wyne, that they maie be vnto vs the bodye and bloude of thy moste dere ly beloued sonne Jesus Christ: who in the same nyght that he was betrayed: tooke bread, and when he had blessed, and geuen thankes: he brake it, and gaue it to his disciples, saiyng: Take, eate, this is my bodye which is geuen for you, do this in remembraunce of me.

2. Holy Communion, *The Booke of the Common Prayer* (London: Edward Whitchurch, 1549), showing printed black crosses, and handwritten ink annotations indicating manual actions and chant by a priest. From the library of John Cosin. Durham University Library, shelf mark: SB+ 0851/1, sig. Y2^v.

What happened in practice varied from parish to parish. One surviving copy of 1549 in Durham University Library reveals small handwritten crosses (see Figure 2), possibly indicating the insertion of additional manual actions. The ink bears witness to how a priest who had been celebrating the Mass in Latin for many years before the legislation was slow to change everything in line with the new text. Other marks in the same copy seem to indicate how he parsed the text in order to chant. For some, then, the English Mass is assimilated as much as possible with the Latin, while for others it became a clean break with the past. By chance, this copy later passed into the possession of Bishop Cosin, who was charged with revising the *Book of Common Prayer* in 1660 (see Chapter 4).

The printers were Richard Grafton (d.1573), the King's Printer, and his business partner Edward Whitchurch (d.1562). Grafton had printed the Communion of 1548; Whitchurch beat him to the post with the new book on 7 March. The effort of the printers in supplying copies for every parish in the country was staggering, and strained their resources.

The new services began immediately to be used in St Paul's Cathedral and evangelical parishes in London. At Worcester, Holy Week followed a truncated version of Sarum, before going over to English on Easter Tuesday (23 April). By Whitsun on 9 June, the *Book of Common Prayer* was compulsory. Cranmer preached a sermon in St Paul's before the city worthies; further sermons followed at Paul's Cross by star preachers such as Miles Coverdale (1488–1569), only to be abandoned on the Wednesday when it was realized that the new Calendar no longer included this day as a festival. In Norwich, English services were enforced immediately; Cranmer sent his preachers into Kent.

Yet there was also trouble in the air. Commotion about the enclosure of common land broke out in Wiltshire, Somerset, and Bristol in May. In Cornwall, the *Book of Common Prayer* became the occasion for outright rebellion. Armed rebels, gathered at Bodmin, agreed a set of articles drawn up by priests. Cranmer's new liturgy was here described as 'a Christmas game', perhaps referring to the rubric that made parishioners line up for Communion by gender, on opposite sides of the chancel, as if (it was said) for a dance. On the day after Whitsun, at Sampford Courtenay in Devon, the priest dressed up 'in his old popish attire and sayeth mass and all such services as in past times accustomed'. By 20 June, this group had joined with the Cornish rebels at Crediton in Devon and begun to lay siege to Exeter. Slow to react at first, Protector Somerset assembled forces in July, and 300 rebels were killed in one day in a battle outside Exeter. The rebels retreated back to Sampford Courtenay until their final defeat in August. Four thousand West Country rebels died in all.

Bucer arrived for work in Cambridge on 8 July, only to wake up the next day to news of commotion. In a letter he reported copies of the new prayer book were burned by rebels. Articles drawn up in Cornwall called for prayers for the dead and a Mass in honour of the Five Wounds of Christ, the symbol of the Pilgrimage of Grace in 1536. Cranmer reacted with contempt. 'Had you rather be like pies [magpies] or parrots, that be taught to speak, and yet understand not one word what they say?' The response was a propaganda war. In London, as martial law was introduced, Cranmer took over St Paul's for the purpose, claiming in the new services to preach pure scripture to true Christian men. He personally led the singing of the Litany, adding a special Collect of repentance for rebellion, and celebrated Communion wearing a cope and silk cap in place of the Eucharistic vestments (see Chapter 4).

Indeed, as so often in times of cultural revolution, the regime responded to opposition by declaring that the revolution had not gone far enough. Altars were destroyed in Norwich during the Bishop's visitations of 1550. Injunctions in other dioceses such as Canterbury and London enforced the use of the new services, and outlawed any remnants of the old, including books. Articles searched out whether any backsliding priests were elevating the host, breathing upon the bread, or ringing the sacring bell; whether parishioners were talking or walking during the English service; whether the youth was carousing or gaming or drinking during church hours; or whether anyone was invoking the saints or maintaining purgatory or images or relics or candles.

The *Book of Common Prayer* revised

Now it was felt that the new *Book of Common Prayer* had compromised too much to meet the misgivings of traditionalists. Early in 1550, Bucer and Peter Martyr, installed as professors at Cambridge and Oxford, made comments on the existing book, with suggestions for a revised version. Bucer's comments survive in two manuscripts, including one in his crabbed, indecipherable handwriting (Corpus Christi College, Cambridge, MS 172).

Bucer by now had attended English services himself. He approved, but feared that much else remained that encouraged superstition. Prime among this was a range of physical gestures, especially at Mass, that could imply a change of nature in physical things,

'as if by magic' (*quasi magica*). The small black crosses used
in the 1549 edition to mark out manual actions by the priest in
Baptism, Marriage, and the Visitation of the Sick, as well as
Communion, should go.

Revising the book, well in hand by the summer of 1550, was given
new urgency by the publication in 1551 of an *Explication and
assertion of the Catholic faith* by Stephen Gardiner (d.1555).
The result was to make the second *Book of Common Prayer* much
more explicit and decisive in its rejection of the real presence.
Parliament debated revision in winter 1551–2, as did Convocation,
the only time when the official governing body of the Church of
England was allowed a say in the making of English liturgy. A new
Act of Uniformity passed in April 1552; new books were printed
once again by Grafton and Whitchurch.

A superficial glance might mistake this for a cut and paste job,
but even in minute detail the effect is a total revamp. Communion
is the prime example. Not only is the word 'canon' dropped, but
its sacred function is remodelled. Christ's words of institution
are followed immediately by the distribution of bread and wine,
without so much as an 'Amen' of ritual mystery. The *Gloria* is
moved to the end, and the biblical readings, intercessions, and
sermon take more prominent positions. The effect overall is to
turn Communion into a rite of penitence. This is matched in
Morning and Evening Prayer by an elaborate opening sequence
of penitential prayers. The Ten Commandments are given pride
of place, and inscribed on the walls of churches, painted over old
images in the rood. For many ministers (the word itself is changed
from 'priests'), the centre of divine worship is the sermon. To mark
this, the stone altar is removed from its permanent place in the
east end of the church, and the centre of gravity is now the pulpit,
near a moveable wooden table in the centre of the nave. Rubrics
instruct parishioners to stand either side, with the minister in
their midst, rather than as before, as the focal point of a miracle
hidden behind a chancel screen.

As a textual fetish showing the sensitivity and controversy of these moves, later editions of the 1552 book contained an insertion, attributed to John Knox (d.1572), known as the 'Black Rubric', because it did not have the 'red letter' approval of the official rubrics (Box 5).

Box 5 The Black Rubric of 1552

Although no ordre can be so perfectlye devised, but it may be of some, eyther for theyr ignoraunce and infermitie, or els of malice and obstinacie, misconstrued, depraved, and interpreted in a wrong part: And yet because brotherly charitie willeth, that so much as conveniently may be, offences shoulde be taken awaye: therefore we willing to doe the same. Whereas it is ordeyned in the booke of common prayer, in the administracion of the Lordes Supper, that the Communicants knelyng shoulde receyve the holye Communion: whiche thynge beyng well mente, for a sygnificacion of the humble and gratefull acknowledgyng of the benefites of Chryst, geven unto the woorthye receyver, and to avoyde the prophanacion and dysordre, which about the holy Communion myght els ensue: Leste yet the same kneelyng myght be thought or taken otherwyse, we dooe declare that it is not ment thereby, that any adoracion is doone, or oughte to bee doone, eyther unto the Sacramentall bread or wyne there bodily receyved, or unto anye reall and essencial presence there beeyng of Christes naturall fleshe and bloude. For as concernynge the Sacramentall bread and wyne, they remayne styll in theyr verye naturall substaunces, and therefore may not be adored, for that were Idolatrye to be abhorred of all faythfull christians. And as concernynge the naturall body and blood of our saviour Christ, they are in heaven and not here. For it is agaynst the trueth of Christes true natural bodye, to be in moe places then in one, at one tyme. (OWC, 667)

It is a strange act of censorship: not so much a change in either text or rubric, as a prohibition on what goes on in the mind of a believer during the sacrament. Kneeling is not disallowed so much as disembodied. It is permitted as a gesture of humility and gratitude, but not of 'adoration'. Bucer called the medieval Eucharist 'bread worship'. In the 1552 text, material things stay where they are: 'as concernynge the naturall body and blood of our saviour Christ, they are in heaven and not here'.

Even so, this extraordinary act of Protestant triumph was short-lived. Edward VI lived less than a year longer, dying in July 1553. Within a month, his sister Mary I had banned the revised English liturgy just as decisively as the old regime had banned the Latin. The strange counterfactual history of the English Reformation begs us to consider what would have happened if she had lived. No doubt England might have remained forever Catholic and European. Instead the relentless turmoil of religious change went on and on. Chapter 3 will describe in detail the nature and theology of the English services and prayers, and also their witness to gesture, faith, and worship.

Chapter 3
Word, body, and gesture

The most widely produced image of prayer in the Western world is Albrecht Dürer's *Betende Hände* or *Praying hands* (now in the Albertina in Vienna). *Praying hands* is found on posters, dishcloths, tea-urns, aprons, coffee mugs, and mobile phones. It is etched into Andy Warhol's tombstone and tattooed on Justin Bieber's left leg. Cliché or not, the drawing represents a yearning for a transcendent image of human prayer in action, seemingly beyond individual confession or even beyond religion. The hands present themselves to us as if disembodied, cut off below the cuffs of the shirt. Both subject and object of the prayer are somehow missing, so that all that is left is the gesture of fingers barely touching each other in rapt concentration, and with it, an aspiration, implied in the gesture, towards a world beyond this present one.

However, this interpretation of Dürer's pen-and-ink drawing is misleading. The provenance of the image is a study for the Heller altarpiece in the Dominican church in Frankfurt-am-Main completed before the Reformation between 1507 and 1509. The hands in their proper context are therefore the opposite of disembodied, and follow a conventional Catholic iconography, devotional and liturgical, of the assumption and coronation of the Virgin Mary. The hands stand therefore between an idea of prayer as personal and spontaneous and one of prayer as formal and ritualistic.

Prayer is not only verbal but is embodied in physical gestures, whether in the hands of Dürer's drawing, or in the body prostrated in the direction of Jerusalem or Mecca, or the near universal human action of kneeling in humility or worship. Such actions might seem to incorporate a universal language of the body, a naturalized semiotics of worship before a deity. Yet at another level, this semiotics is anything but natural: it is conventional, and works by means of a system of recognition within a social code of performance. At times of religious conflict or change, such ritual actions become the object of acute concern. As we have seen, the performance of prayer caused intense scrutiny at the Reformation. At its most basic this is a quarrel between the demands of body and mind. Yet the *Book of Common Prayer* shows it to be much more complex.

This chapter examines the contents of the *Book of Common Prayer* in intimate detail. The *Book of Common Prayer* is a book not only of prayer, narrowly conceived, but also of ritual: a corpus of gestures, practices, and performances. Mankind is a 'ceremonial animal', Ludwig Wittgenstein once said. Rituals, anthropology tells us, are what make the human animal different. Bowing, kneeling, kissing, the laying on of hands, are basic not only to religious worship but also to the human expression of relationship. This chapter examines how the *Book of Common Prayer*, while rejecting so many of the physical forms of the medieval rites, creates its own grammar of social action. In order to understand this, special attention will be paid to the book's rubrics, and how they changed from edition to edition, from 1549 to 1552 and afterwards.

Recent psychology has invented a concept known as 'body memory'. The science is disputed, as there are no known means by which tissues other than the brain are capable of storing memories. And yet it is easy to apply the idea at least in metaphoric form to religious ritual. In prayer, the body remembers what to do: it kneels or stands as if by instinct. During the Reformation, this is compounded by the way that the body had to learn new gestures, and inhibit others, in order to conform with new government policy on doctrine. However, the body does not forget so easily. Embodied within the surviving objects, images, and texts of the period, we find contested means of remembering and forgetting all kinds of forms of devotion.

Examples can be found in three things that are barely present in the *Book of Common Prayer*: music, bells, and bowing. And yet the residual form of these suppressed aspects survived the Reformation. Medieval liturgy had a rich musical heritage, for smaller churches as well as large foundations and monasteries. The *Book of Common Prayer* from 1549 contains many rubrics which indicate singing by a choir, and music is obviously permitted, if not encouraged. Yet it contains not one note of music. The lack was made up by the *Book of Common Prayer Noted* by John Marbeck (or Merbecke) in 1550, but this book was never reprinted after the 1552 revision. Nonetheless, cathedrals and collegiate churches retained organs and employed choirs in the Elizabethan period, and even small parish churches for centuries used the Metrical Psalms (1562) of Thomas Sternhold and John Hopkins.

Church bells date back to Norman times. They were used in monasteries to sound the hours of prayer, and in parishes to announce the *Ave Maria*, Matins and Evensong, or the Mass of the dead. The 'chime' or 'peal' summoned worshippers to church; the 'passing bell' called them to pray for the departed; the 'death knell' to signal a death in the parish. The *Book of Common Prayer* mentions bells only once, in a most obscure place (the service for Ash Wednesday). Controversial as they were, bells continued to be part of everyday church life, marking key moments in divine service. Surviving bell inscriptions show that the 'passing bell' was used at funerals to summon to the grave, despite changes in the burial service itself. Indeed, in time, Protestant England became home to one of the most distinctive traditions of church bells anywhere in the world, 'change ringing', symbolic of the church in the community to the present day.

Bowing is a further sign, in a world of human gesture, of the obscure legacy of memory in religious performance. Kneeling is commonplace in Protestant traditions, as in Catholic. However, bowing the head, specifically at the name of Jesus, became anathema to Puritans in the 17th century. Equally, Laudians (see Chapter 4) adopted the practice as a habit which declared their own orthodoxy. Yet it is never enjoined anywhere in the *Book of Common Prayer*. It survived the Reformation, like an amputated limb, a bodily movement frozen in time from medieval practice.

Text and rubric

What is a 'book of common prayer'? The title that Cranmer's church gave to the official English liturgy for the next 450 years is beguilingly simple but contained two controversial ideas. The word 'common' countered the 'diverse' practices of the medieval church. The church began in a single unity with Christ, Cranmer says in his preface. One people will now pray from one book. This ideal was designed not only with evangelical theology in mind, but also with Tudor polity (see Chapter 4). However, a deeply felt issue also lurks in the seemingly unexceptionable word 'prayer'. The new book asks fundamental questions about what prayer is, what it is for, and how it works.

Prayer is mentioned frequently in scripture. Seth 'calls upon' the Lord in Genesis 4:26; the Old Testament is full of similar expressions: to intercede, mediate, consult, or beseech. Perhaps the commonest association is to 'cry out to' God, as in the Psalms. Praying in the New Testament in Greek is ubiquitous. The central example is of course the Lord's Prayer, which occurs twice in the gospels: in Matthew, where it is part of the sermon on the mount (6:9–13) and a shorter form in Luke (11:2–4). Furthermore, prayer occasionally suggests highly complex psychological processes, such as in Romans 8:26: 'Likewise the Spirit also helpeth our infirmities: for we know not what we should pray for as we ought: but the Spirit itself maketh intercession for us with groanings which cannot be uttered.' Or else Jesus' own words at Gethsemane: 'And he went a little further, and fell on his face, and prayed, saying, O my Father, if it be possible, let this cup pass from me: nevertheless not as I will, but as thou wilt' (Matt. 26:39).

The Lord's Prayer is introduced by Jesus as the paradigm for all prayer ('After this manner therefore pray ye') (Matt. 6:9). In contrast, Jesus also sets out a series of admonitions about how *not* to pray. 'But when ye pray, use not vain repetitions, as the heathen do: for they think that they shall be heard for their much speaking' (Matt. 6:7). Between these positive and negative modes lay room for argument. Medieval ritual, as we saw in Chapter 1, radiated outwards from the Mass. Individual prayers stud the Mass as they do in all parts of the Sarum rites: varying between forms of physical enactment and elements of personal or collective petition. Underlying all of these structures lay a system of prayer for a religious life as expressed most clearly in monasteries.

The initial move in Protestant reforms of prayer was negative. Protestant culture reverberates with antipathy to bodily practice and to prayer by rote. In this, Jesus' strictures against 'vain repetitions' in Matthew 6 are invoked again and again. Many also spoke out against Latin, implying it was a form of mumbo jumbo, incompatible with the idea of sincere adherence. This might suggest an alternative model of prayer as both improvisatory on the one hand, and strictly verbal on the other. Yet it is immediately obvious from the text of the 1549 *Book of Common Prayer* that this is not the case. It consists of verbal forms, spoken aloud rather than thought internally, and shared by a community that recognizes them as standard. And its rubrics reiterate again and again that prayer is not only verbal. Indeed, a first obvious point about the *Book of Common Prayer* is that it shifts the emphasis of what rubrics are for. Rubrics in a missal were in red because they defined the physical actions of the priest during the Mass. The rubrics of the *Book of Common Prayer* are aimed just as much at the congregation.

Protestant commentaries on the Lord's Prayer from early in the Reformation declared that words of prayer are ineffective unless felt in the heart. Bucer in Straßburg in 1527 insisted this was true not only of private prayers but of formal and public rituals in church. Even in public prayer, every word must be meant by every person, and meaning is authenticated by affective experience. Bucer inveighs against *Torpor orandi*, saying the words in a stupor, or saying obscure words in a form of magical jargon. This is followed by a conventional attack on intercession of the saints, prayers for the dead, and other vulgar errors. It is underscored by the replacement of rubrics of correct performance by the priest, with rules of emotional engagement for the laity: *Quid enim aliud est orare sine desiderio, & gratias agere sine sensu beneficii, quam gaudere sine gaudio, dolere sine dolore?* ('For what is praying without desire, or giving thanks without a feeling of gratitude, than rejoicing without joy, or weeping without suffering?').

Some historians have argued that the effect of the Reformation was to replace the social mystery of the Mass with a didactic system of instruction in which religion became whatever could be taught and learned. This underestimates the extent to which Protestantism was concerned with sincerity above knowledge. Faith, as well as a list of beliefs, is an ideal of feeling, without which faith is meaningless. Protestants continued to pray in a petitionary form, asking God to intervene in their lives. In this they followed a principle stated in Erasmus's 1524 treatise on prayer: 'nothing forbids us from revealing our feelings to God in whatever words we wish'. Prayer, Jean Calvin (1509–64) says (borrowing from Bucer), is a form of *colloquium* or conversation with God. As in Luther, prayer is an extension of the gift of faith, guaranteeing God's promises. To achieve this, the mind must be 'free from carnal cares and thoughts by which it can be called or led away from right and pure contemplation of God'.

However, as well as negative freedom from distraction, this means a positive education in the emotions: 'the only persons who duly and properly gird themselves to pray are those who are so moved by God's majesty that freed from earthly cares and affections they come to it'. Significantly, Calvin says here that it is proper and natural for the ardour of prayer to find bodily expression: 'the rite of raising the hands means that men remember that they are far removed from God unless they raise their thoughts on high'; for this reason the Psalmist is said to 'lift up my soul'. Kneeling signifies devotion; knocking of the breast true penitence.

Holy Communion

In 1549, many aspects of the service for Communion appeared at least as traditional in form. The priest continued to wear a white robe ('alb') covered with a chasuble (a circular garment with a hole for the head). The outline structure followed the sequence of invariable elements from the Mass, although now translated into English: the *Kyrie* ('Lord have mercie upon us'); *Gloria* ('Glory be to God on high'); the Nicene Creed; the *Sanctus* ('Holy, holy, holy'); *Benedictus* ('Blessed is he', a song of welcome for Christ on Palm Sunday); and *Agnus Dei* ('O lambe of god', after the consecration and distribution of the bread and wine). All these elements contained provisos allowing singing by a choir. Crucially, the text contained a version of the Canon, the most solemn part of the Mass, called 'a full, perfect, and sufficient sacrifyce, oblacion, and satysfaccyon'. At the moment of consecration, the text contained small black crosses (✠) to signify that the priest was to perform a manual action such as making the sign of the cross in the air or on his body, similar to places in a missal where a red cross serves the same purpose.

The wording and conduct of the service show the result of different factions in clergy and parliament in the debates of 1548. The word 'Canon' is used even though it had been called an 'abomination' by Luther in 1525. The word 'sacrifyce' is used in one place, but is substituted in another by 'commemoracion', articulating Zwingli's doctrine of Communion as a memorial performance rather than renewed enactment. The word *oblatio*, meaning 'offering to God', was one of the most sacred words in the Latin liturgy, and made it into the 1549 service, even though it had been rejected by a committee of bishops beforehand. This shows the extreme sensitivity of language surrounding the mystery of the Eucharist. The Latin rite compared the sacrifice made by Christ on the cross with the offering of the host in the Mass; the 1549 text used the word but left interpretation open.

On other points, the 1549 Communion was more openly radical. The priest was to make the consecration of bread and wine 'without any elevacion, or shewing the Sacrament to the people' (OWC, 31). This was the highpoint of the Roman rite, as we saw in Chapter 1. For many, forbidding the elevation of the host removed its spiritual benefit. On the other hand, however, the English Communion enjoined the administration of the sacrament to the whole congregation, and explicitly 'in both kindes' (OWC, 34). This was a rallying point of the Reformation.

Here we uncover the ambiguity of the new service. It proclaimed a new kind of participation for the laity. As each parishioner received Communion, the priest promised that it would 'preserve thy bodye and soule unto everlasting lyfe' (OWC, 34). These words were translated directly from Sarum, but it was no longer clear what they meant, theologically. At one point, the service uses a careful expression, 'spiritually eate'. This was a bone of contention well before 1549. Used positively, it lent the idea that Communion does more than commemorate scripture, in making the one who receives it into a different person. But Thomas More in 1533 declared that it also took something away: if we eat 'spiritually' then we do not eat the body of Christ *in fact*. At stake in all these variations of words is the very idea of the real presence of Christ in the sacrament.

In truth, 1549 appeared to please neither side properly. The 1552 revision of Holy Communion was unapologetically radical and comprehensive. The vernacular Canon, achieved at such cost, was split in three, and the word removed. The first part, Intercession, was put early in the service; Consecration was altered and ended abruptly; the third, Oblation, was removed until after the Communion of the people.

These changes were not incidental: they altered the character of the service. Innovation is made explicit by opening the service not with the *Kyrie* but the Ten Commandments. The new service frames the sacrament in terms that are catechistical and penitential. Communion reinforces the doctrinal message of Christianity, emphasizing the centrality of faith in the gospel, and repentance for sinfulness. Confession by means of public display precedes Communion itself. As for consecration, the black crosses are eliminated along with gestures by the priest in bowing to the bread or wine, or moving them from place to place. As the elements are administered, any inference of real presence disappears: 'Take and eate this, in remembraunce that Christ died for thee, and fede on him in thy heart by faith, with thankesgevyng' (OWC, 137).

Nonetheless, gesture remained a sensitive register to the most mysterious parts of the ritual. In 1552, the people are to kneel right at the beginning of Communion, in order to show repentance, as the Ten Commandments are publicly rehearsed (see OWC, 125). As the congregation gathers to receive Communion, the priest tells them to do so 'mekely knelynge upon your knees' (OWC, 134). This posture is retained for the general confession. As such, kneeling is associated with penitence, and passes the Protestant test of gesture as a signal of sincerity. However, as the people gather with the priest at the 'borde' (the Communion Table), another rubric provides that the bread be delivered 'to the people in their handes kneling' (OWC, 137). Kneeling here ambiguates between worship, and something like veneration.

As described in Chapter 2, this became the occasion for the additional 'Black Rubric'. This reduced the bodily performance of kneeling to 'a sygnificacion of the humble and gratefull acknowledgyng of the benefites of Chryst' (OWC, 667). Yet the prescription was controversial, and eliminated in 1559 in the Elizabethan edition of the book. For a century afterwards (and beyond), kneeling at Communion became an open sore: enforced by bishops in visitations (more pressingly from the 1620s on), and passionately rejected by Puritans. It was with prophetic care that Cranmer added 'Certayne Notes' about ritual performance in 1549: 'As touching kneeling, crossing, holding up of handes, knocking upon the brest, and other gestures: they may be used or left as every mans devocion serveth without blame' (OWC, 97). Such tolerant indifference to human gesture turned out to be an empty promise.

As significant as verbal changes to text and rubric in 1552 were alterations to vestments (see Chapter 4), ornaments, and church furniture. Altars in the chancel were replaced by a table in the nave. The parish, instead of witnessing Mass from afar, behind a screen, took Communion shoulder to shoulder with the minister, in plain sight, as if gathered for a meal. The bread was to be 'the beste and purest wheate breade, that conveniently may be gotten' (OWC, 140), changed from a 1549 rubric requiring wafers.

One aspect of material culture shows the ambiguity especially well. In 1558, new Visitation Articles under Queen Elizabeth continued the zeal under Edward VI to destroy images of 'feigned and false miracles, pilgrimages, idolatry and superstition'. Included were items of church furniture associated with the Mass. Reports told of sacring bells 'hung about a calf's neck' or 'at a horse's ear', and holy water vats turned into a swine's trough. However, other Injunctions reasserted propriety.

In 1569, Archbishop Parker's articles in the diocese of Canterbury enquired 'Whether they do minister in any prophane cuppes, bowles, dishes, or chalices heretofore used at masse or els in a decent Communion cuppe provided and kept for the same purpose only'. The articles of Archbishop Grindal in 1576 asked 'Whether you have in your Parish Churches and Chapels, a fair and comely Communion Cup of Silver, and a Cover of Silver for the same, which may serve also for the ministration of the Communion Bread'. The new orders reflected the larger vessels necessitated by ministering wine to the laity. Figure 3 shows an example of a new 'decent Communion cuppe' from Rufforth,

3. **Elizabethan Communion Cup. Hallmarked: York, 1570.**

near York, hallmarked 1570. A medieval chalice may have been melted down to make it. The cover here could also serve, as Grindal advised, as a dish to distribute the Communion Bread.

Morning and Evening Prayer

A paradox lurks in the attitude of the *Book of Common Prayer* to Communion. The insistence that all the parish take Communion in both kinds is balanced by the fact that available parish records show that purchase of wine is not commensurate with regular practice of Holy Communion. Indeed, in many parishes, Communion took place only once a year at Easter, in continuation of medieval practice. Reformed theologians urged more regular enforcement, such as monthly Communion, but the evidence suggests that in practice this meant only a number of extra occasions around Easter.

An unintended consequence is that Morning and Evening Prayer, which initially had the character of a residue of the monastic divine office, became the staple of English church worship. Indeed, only in the late 20th century, when experiments in liturgical reform coincided with a revival of interest in ancient forms of the Eucharist, did Holy Communion become the centrepiece of parish life that had always been professed. Some bishops in the 1560s envisaged a Great Service in which Morning Prayer, the Litany, and Holy Communion would continue seamlessly in a two- or three-hour demonstration of devotion. Yet apart from cathedrals and large collegiate churches (which had the resources and choirs to realize this), this remained only an ideal. Parishes used Morning Prayer, perhaps with an Ante-Communion, supplemented by a sermon. Where the minister was unqualified to preach, an official *Book of Homilies*, full of Tudor admonitions to civil obedience, sufficed in its place.

Morning Prayer was entitled Matins in 1549, showing its medieval origins, but began with several features that immediately proclaimed its Reformed character. The priest begins by saying the Lord's Prayer 'with a loude voyce' (OWC, 7); in Sarum the prayer is inaudible and addressed internally. In Sarum this is followed by *Ave Maria*; in 1549 this is silently excised. In other respects the 1549 service showed a respect for tradition: after Psalm 95, sung at the opening of the office since the earliest times, a sequence of psalms and scriptural lessons follows, with permission for the gospel to be sung rather than read. Then come two hymns, the *Te Deum* and the *Benedicite*. These are the only sources in the 1549 *Book of Common Prayer* that do not come from canonical scripture.

Although these hymns survive in 1552, indeed come down to the 20th century as the epitome of English parish worship, in other respects the service was carefully revised away from its monastic origins. The service now began with a series of sentences from scripture to set a penitential mood for the mixed congregation. After 1552, this was followed by the 'generall confession', shown in Box 6 in the version of 1559.

Box 6 The General Confession at Morning Prayer in 1559

Almightie and moste merciful father, we have erred and straied from thy waies, lyke lost shepe. We have folowed too much the devises and desires of our owne hartes. We have offended against thy holy lawes. We have left undone those thinges whiche we ought to have done, and we have done those thinges which we ought not to have done, and there is no health in us: but thou, O Lorde, have mercy upon us miserable offendours. Spare thou them O God, whiche confesse their faultes. Restore thou them that be penitent, accordyng to thy promises declared unto mankynde, in Christe Jesu our Lorde. And graunt, O moste merciful father, for his sake, that we may hereafter lyve a godly, ryghtuous, and sobre life, to the glory of thy holy name. Amen. (OWC, 103–4)

The congregation thus begins its devotion kneeling, a physical gesture that embodies collective penitence. The wording is original to 1552 (although a shorter form of confession had been used in Communion in 1549), and is recited clause by clause, following the lead of the minister. Afterwards comes an absolution 'to be pronounced by the Minister alone' (see OWC, 104). Only now comes the sequence, beginning with the Lord's Prayer, which opened the 1549 rite. Public collective repentance frames the service, and the Lord's Prayer, the hymns, and the Creed flow out from this. This was a clear mark of sincerity in faith. Yet as always there lurked the danger of ritual. By making the minister alone give voice to forgiveness in absolution, the suspicion was raised among radical Protestants that the service reinvented a form of magical superstition.

The service ends with three Collects, both in 1549 and in 1552. The first of these varied from week to week, and was also used in the Communion service. The form of the Collect (although dating back to the 6th century) has come to be associated especially with the *Book of Common Prayer*. By tradition, Cranmer is believed to have taken special care in composing them, and they are considered the pinnacle of his liturgical writing.

A 'collect' derives from an idea that the priest speaks on collective behalf of the people. It usually consists of a single grammatical unit, containing a petition, often referring to Christ's mediation in the life of the congregation, ending in a statement of praise. English primers before 1549 contained a variety of often clumsy versions of old Latin Collects. Cranmer undertook a full-scale revision, sometimes translating literally from the Latin, sometimes adapting, and sometimes making new compositions (there are twenty-four of these, mostly for saints' days). The Collects are grouped together in a special section of the book, alongside the gospels and epistles for every Sunday and holy day.

Even among Cranmer's borrowings we see his originality, such as the 'Prayer of St Chrysostom' taken from Byzantine liturgy. This he transformed into an English classic: 'whan two or three bee gathered in they name, thou wylt graunt theyr requestes' (OWC, 45). An example of Cranmer's original composition is the Collect for the First Sunday in Advent, the beginning of the church year. This survives word for word in 1662, when it was decided to say it every day in Advent until Christmas Eve (Box 7).

Morning Prayer finished with two unvarying Collects, 'for Peace' and 'for Grace'. Evening Prayer was much shorter, and changed little in 1552. It began with the Lord's Prayer and followed this with scriptural passages in sung form: the *Magnificat* (sung by the pregnant Virgin to her cousin Elizabeth in the gospel of Luke); and *Nunc Dimittis* (which Simeon sings, also in Luke, when he is finally allowed to die having seen Jesus). These had been sung (respectively) at Vespers and Compline since the earliest Western liturgies. Tradition was mixed with reform in 1552, with the introduction of the Creed, emphasizing collective faith. Like Matins, Evensong ended with three Collects: the collect for the day, followed by two special prayers for night time, 'Lyghten our darkenes we beseche thee, O lord, & by thy great mercy defende us from all perilles and daungers of thys nyght' (OWC, 16).

Box 7 Cranmer's Collect for the First Sunday in Advent (from the edition of 1662)

Almighty God, give us grace that we may cast away the works of darkness, and put upon us the armour of light now in the time of this mortal life (in which thy Son Jesus Christ came to visit us in great humility;) that in the last day, when he shall come again in his glorious Majesty, to judge both the quick and the dead, we may rise to the life immortal, through him who liveth and reigneth with thee and the Holy Ghost, now and ever. *Amen.* (OWC, 271)

Morning and Evening Prayer thus set out a form of daily and weekly collective worship, which rivalled and in time eclipsed Holy Communion. It set a rhythm for devotion in line with the passage of the day and of the seasons. Its tone was earnest and communal, emphasizing the central place of faith and penitence in the Christian life. Prayer is aimed at a godly order of life. This took on a decidedly national character.

Nowhere was this in more plain view than in the Litany. The Litany, a usefully flexible form of processional in the medieval church, was an afterthought in 1549, placed after the Communion and with no obvious function except that it must *not* be processional. In 1552 it found its role, prescribed for use on Sundays, Wednesdays, and Fridays. The Litany now became a ready-made additional service dedicated to collective penitence.

It enforced aspects of doctrine, but also contained fulsome prayer (and a little praise by proxy) for the monarch. The monarch is made synonymous with 'the true worshipping' of God 'in righteousnes and holynes of lyfe' (OWC, 118). Supporting the monarch is woven into the structure of national religious life, down through bishops and pastors, to secular lords and councillors, and thence to magistrates and people. The nation prays together, works together, suffers together. At the same time, the godly nation hopes for protection from its enemies. These come from within, from pride and envy but also from fornication and the flesh; and without, from war, plague, and famine, but also from sedition and conspiracy. This decidedly ideological edge to prayer in 1549 and 1552 included escape 'from the tyrannye of the bishop of Rome and all his detestable enormities' (OWC, 41), until Mary I eliminated it. Elizabeth I did not restore it in the 1559 version. Nevertheless, the Litany explicitly asks God's blessing on the social and political status quo.

Baptism and Confirmation

This completed the parts of the *Book of Common Prayer* set aside for everyday worship. However, it also contained services for special occasions, replacing what in the medieval church were contained in the Manual, a book for the use of the priest. For the church presided over the rites of passage in life (baptism, marriage, burial, and so on):

> Birth, and copulation and death.
> That's all, that's all, that's all, that's all.

So T. S. Eliot wrote in *Sweeney Agonistes* in 1927, the year he converted to Anglicanism. For the rest of his life the *Book of Common Prayer* was his constant companion. It was in these occasional services that the book entered the soul of the nation, since even people who rejected the official church for other purposes, and refused to attend its services, would christen their children or get married to its words. This is why it is phrases from these parts of the book ('till death us do part') that remain most familiar.

Baptism has a claim to be the oldest Christian ritual, as Christ himself is baptized in the gospel accounts. These scriptural origins ensured that of all rituals this was the least problematic among early Protestants. However, since early Christian times, a debate existed about whether, as with Christ, baptism should take place in adulthood, or whether—since performance of the rite was considered essential for salvation—infants should be baptized as close to birth as possible.

In 1523, Thomas Müntzer, previously a follower of Luther, banned infant baptism in Allstedt in Saxony. During the Peasants' War in 1525 Müntzer's troops were defeated and he was executed. Anabaptism (meaning literally 'baptizing again' adults with a full confession of faith) continued to be a point of issue throughout the next centuries, and was ruthlessly excluded by the official English church. Baptizing infants warded off the opposite fear, that a baby who died unbaptized would be damned.

A service for Private Baptism was written into the first versions of the *Book of Common Prayer*, implying permission for emergency baptism by midwives. However, for the 1604 version, James I desired this to be removed, since (he said with his gift for charity) a woman could no more baptize than an ape. This created a loophole in social practice which caused desperate measures up to late Victorian times. In Thomas Hardy's *Tess of the d'Urbervilles* (1891), Tess agonizes that she cannot give her baby Sorrow a burial since she performed the baptism herself.

The *Book of Common Prayer* took some of the sting out of these debates by emphasizing Confirmation. While ridding it of sacramental status, Protestants from Luther onwards used Confirmation as a way of making Christian education, called 'catechism', a central aim of the church. Luther and Calvin both wrote popular forms of catechism, and while the 1549 prayer book version is much simpler than these, its use was supplemented by a range of similar texts. Confirmation could thus be used as a complement to the infant rite of baptism.

But baptism remained controversial, because of its roots in the medieval practice of exorcism, in which the devil is expelled using a series of bodily acts. In the Sarum Manual, the priest breathed on the candidate at the door of the church; salt was placed in the mouth to remove the corruption of sin; the ears and lips were anointed with spittle. This last was a ritual called *ephphatha* (after Jesus's command in Aramaic, Mark 7: 34, 'be opened'). The white robe worn by the baby, signing the infant with the cross, unction with oil on breast and back, and giving a candle or taper, were all material customs embedded into the sacrament, alongside ritual immersion by water.

Reformers wished to cut away such 'superstitions' (as they saw them) from the simplicity of the scriptural action. However, successful performance of baptism was associated popularly with the elaborate sequence of ritual processes. Holy words and gestures held objective power; baptismal water was kept separate, and considered to have magical powers; the 'chrisom' or cloth for the anointment of the child was retained by the priest; godparents washed their hands to ensure none of the holy oil (or 'chrism') used in blessing the baptismal water remained. Since the ceremony ensured the safety, through eternity, of the child, every aspect of ritual caused friction as change took place. Arguments around these rituals continued for centuries. The *ephphatha* was removed from the 1549 service. Exorcism was retained, but in 1552 was eliminated. Triple immersion of the baby was enjoined in 1549, but in 1552 this was reduced to once.

However, the sign of the cross was still made on the forehead of the infant even in 1552. Along with kneeling at Communion, signing the cross retained more power to move and disturb than any other gesture in the *Book of Common Prayer*. Like kneeling, the gesture contained a powerful conundrum of signification. What does it mean to mark the cross upon the body? Laurence Chaderton wrote a memorandum on signing the cross in about 1600, walking a theological tightrope. Chaderton was Master of Emmanuel College, Cambridge, a Puritan foundation (John Harvard of Massachusetts studied there). A Presbyterian, Chaderton stayed within the establishment; he argued that 'to make signes or representations of spirituall thinges pertains only to god', and could be taken to contravene the second commandment. Yet such actions can be useful and edifying if understood doctrinally, not ritually. By the time of his death at the age of over a hundred in 1640, signing with the cross separated orthodoxy from radicalism.

Participation and *mimesis*

Within these arguments we reach the heart of ritual. In modernity, Mary Douglas complained in *Natural Symbols* (1970), ritual has become a dirty word, implying someone 'who performs external gestures without inner commitment to the ideas and values being expressed'. Recent anthropology has reclaimed the world of ritual. Roy Rappaport, in his last work, *Ritual and Religion in the Making of Humanity* (1999), called it 'the social act basic to humanity'. Duffy's *Stripping of the Altars* mirrored such arguments in calling the Roman Mass 'far more than the object of individual devotion, a means of forgiveness and sanctification: it was the source of human community'.

Rappaport uses an analogy from the world of theatre to make a powerful distinction about ritual. Theatre depends on *mimesis*, on a set of assumptions that the world it is watching is figurative. Audiences, he says, 'do not participate in the performance: they *watch* and they *listen*'. They are clear, that is, about what is representation and what is real. The defining relationship of ritual, by contrast, is 'participation'. In ritual, Rappaport says, participants are bound together in function and in space. They do not observe, they *do*.

In this as in other respects, the *Book of Common Prayer* was caught between worlds. It excluded the more obviously apotropaic aspects of medieval prayer, averting evil influences or bad luck. Protestants shuddered at commonplace practices in which holy bread was used as an amulet, carried on the person to drive off evil events, or placed in the ground to aid a harvest. However, the new Collects were petitionary, and included a prayer for rain, which sounds just like a medieval charm.

An ambiguous case in point is the Solemnization of Marriage in the *Book of Common Prayer*. At the crucial point in the ceremony, each partner is asked (in this case of the female): 'Wilt thou have this man to thy wedded houseband, to live together after Goddes ordeinaunce, in the holy estate of matrimonie?' (OWC, 65). And she replies, if she wants to, 'I will'. In the 20th century, in the US Presbyterian Church, this came to be replaced with 'I do', which makes the point all the more clearly. A person who says this, by the mere act of saying it, becomes married. The philosopher J. L. Austin called this an example of a 'performative utterance', and distinguished successful performance precisely by reference to theatre. Rosalind in Shakespeare's *As You Like It* (4.1.120) pretends to say the vow, but the actors are not thereby committed to live together.

Cranmer anticipated these worries, paying special attention to marriage (perhaps from personal experience). He happily incorporated medieval English vows used in Sarum: 'to have and to holde from this day forwarde, for better, for wurse, for richer, for poorer, in sickenes, and in health' (OWC, 66). Dropping the requirement in Sarum for the wife to promise to be 'bonere and buxom in bedde and at the borde', he added a new phrase 'to love and to cherishe'. Prudishness is joined here to vows that are more social contract than ritual performance. The use of rings, however, was allowed, which soon caused anxieties among Puritans. The social burden of the marriage rite left an imprint as great as any in the *Book of Common Prayer*, familiar from Charlotte Brontë's *Jane Eyre* (1847): 'The marriage cannot go on: I declare the existence of an impediment.'

In *Of Ceremonies*, a supplement to the book that survives in the 1662 version, Cranmer attempts a theoretical solution to the problem of ritual. But the section divides against itself. While Cranmer acknowledges that ceremony originates at the beginnings of Christian tradition, he also sees it at the heart of current quarrels. He draws a line between good and bad ceremony: 'some at the first were of godly intent and purpose devised, and yet at length turned to vanity and superstition'

(OWC, 214). But how can the line be maintained? Christ's gospel, he says in a wonderful phrase, 'is a Religion to serve God, not in bondage of the figure or shadow, but in the freedom of the Spirit'. Yet who by now, in the trauma of the reconstructed Communion, can any more tell 'figure' from 'Spirit'? Cranmer asserts a difference between rituals of the past that 'were most abused' and those in the present that 'are retained for a discipline and order'. But history proved this confidence to be misplaced.

Death and ceremony

If Communion is the most open scene of this conflict, the dead caused the heaviest social burden. Attitudes to the dead were the most fraught of all religious conflicts of the 16th and 17th centuries. The indulgence crisis in 1517 itself concerned the granting (and selling) of pardons to reduce the term in purgatory of a deceased relative. This dispute over sin and penance directly threatened traditional practices, which were also the source of strong emotional attachment.

Purgatory was quickly abolished in the English Reformation, and tombs and charnel houses were desecrated; the dissolution of the monasteries involved the dispersal of dead as well as living inmates. *The Book of Common Prayer* radically transformed the elaborate medieval formation of the Office of the Dead, but contained traces of the old. There was a rite for the Visitation of the Sick, which removed the sacrament of Extreme Unction, but still included Communion for the dying. In the Order for Burial in 1549, the minister spoke directly to the corpse, as if still present: 'I commend thy soule to God the father almighty, and thy body to the grounde, earth to earth, asshes to asshes, dust to dust, in sure and certayne hope of resurreccion to eternall life' (OWC, 82–3).

In 1552 every vestige of the presence of the dead was removed, as if eliminating the body from its own funeral. Prayers for the dead are forbidden, and the whole reduced to the barest possible ceremony of putting a body in the ground, plus an exhortation to good living among those left behind. In *Oliver Twist* (1838), Charles Dickens (1812–70) has Mr Sowerberry cram a burial service from the prayer book into four minutes flat.

However, remembering the dead continued to arouse strong feelings. Reformed funerals often exceeded the strict letter of the prayer book. Local rituals survived the new theology: bells continued to be tolled; the corpse might be met at the boundary of the church. Passage between this world and the next was closely observed. To see the passion in these rites, we need look no further than Shakespeare's *Hamlet*, in which a ghost comes back from the medieval past to haunt a young man trained in Luther's university of Wittenberg. Young Hamlet trades in a new theology of death, based on penitential rituals of self-analysis, putting off the memorial enactment embodied in his father's injunction, 'Remember me' (1.5.91). Old Hamlet nonetheless talks back, and an audience wonders who (and how) it is hearing. Later (4.5.174), Ophelia uses rosemary at the funeral of her father ('There's rosemary, that's for remembrance'), but the priest at her funeral can only use 'Shards, flints and pebbles' (5.1.198), since she is presumed a suicide.

Funerals continued in life in their own way, with mortal paradoxes afflicting English faith for centuries. In the 1650s, Cosin, exiled in Paris from Commonwealth England, lamented that his son was denied a proper burial in Catholic France, his last rites scarcely more elaborate than a dog's. In 1662, Cosin restored a little ceremony to the order for the Burial of the Dead in the new version of the *Book of Common Prayer*.

Chapter 4
Politics and religion

Until recently it was commonplace to assume that a prayer book in the English vernacular, as with the Bible, was an act of popularization and even democratization. Such an idea inscribes itself in the title of the book, the *Book of Common Prayer*. Such appears to be the principle expressed in Cranmer's preface. St Paul wanted the language used in church to be one a congregation can understand and profit from. However:

> the service in this Churche of England (these many yeares) hath been read in Latin to the people, whiche they understoode not, so that they have heard with theyr eares onely; and their hartes, spirite and minde, haue not been edified thereby. (OWC, 4)

Cranmer explicitly appeals to broadening the reach of liturgy, opening it out to a wider audience and a popular register. 'Common prayer' appears to mean 'for the commons', for the people as a whole rather than for an élite of learned readers and listeners.

Diversity and uniformity

However, it needs to be recalled that the *Book of Common Prayer*, as well as a radical reformation of devotion, was a political act of religion. It was brought into being by an Act of Uniformity in Parliament on 21 January 1549. Every time a new version of the book appeared, in 1552, in 1559, and in 1662, a new Act was created, authorizing the book, making it the *only* permitted form of religious ritual and public prayer.

In January 1549, Parliament was unsentimental in its stated aim, 'Unyformytie of Service and Admynistracion of the Sacramentes throughout the Realme'. It lamented 'diverse formes of commen prayer' that prevailed previously. This refers to the different Uses of Latin liturgy, such as Sarum (see Chapter 1). Even worse, Parliament notes that multiform liturgies of the medieval church have multiplied further in the confusions following the Reformation of the 1530s. Now, it appears, virtually anything goes:

> besides the same nowe of late muche more diverse and sondrie fourmes and facions have bene used in the Cathedrall and parishe Churches of Englande and Wales, aswell concernynge the Mattens or mornynge prayer and the Evensong, as also concerninge the Hollie Comunyon comonlie called the Masse, with diverse and sondrie rytes and ceremonyes concerninge the same, and in the admynistracion of other Sacramentes of the Churche.

'Diversity' here has a very different meaning from modern usage, where it might suggest a welcome form of inclusiveness. In Tudor eyes, it is the worst kind of political vice.

Inclusiveness required instead uniformity. The English Reformation was founded on twin pillars of supremacy and succession. The Act of 1534 declared that the king was 'the only supreme head on Earth of the Church of England' and that the Crown shall enjoy 'all honours, dignities, preeminences, jurisdictions, privileges, authorities, immunities, profits, and commodities to the said dignity'. To reinforce the Act, a mandatory oath required all subjects to swear allegiance to monarch and religion.

Using such authority, the king reformed doctrine as he pleased. The king's pleasure shifted in different directions, some Protestant, some conservative. His will allowed the English Bible to be printed in an official version (the 'Great Bible') in 1539, even though translations had been outlawed as recently as 1530. However, the king's religious discretion was hard to read. Within a year came the executions both of More, for refusing to swear the oath; and Tyndale, author of an English version of the Bible that Henry was soon to sanction, for heresy. For the moment, Henry did not touch the liturgy, and retained a personal fondness for Latin ritual books. Cranmer meanwhile bided his time.

Nonetheless, when Cranmer complained in 1549 that the people in experiencing the old Latin Mass 'have heard with theyr eares onely', he is not thinking of democracy. He means that if the text is not understood, it cannot be internalized properly. In that event, it cannot be felt as true faith. In that sense his religion is more exclusive than inclusive. The *Book of Common Prayer* demanded conformity as well as uniformity. It required the right kind of religious feeling, the correct form of faith, correct doctrine, the right spirit of penitence, or of piety and devotion.

Of course, the idea of a national religious consensus was a fiction. Indeed the first person the Privy Council found itself having to deal with for contravening the king's uniform orders of service was the king's own sister. The Lord Protector's agents passed information on Mary to the Council on 16 June 1549, within a week of the new Prayer Book becoming the official use at Pentecost on 9 June. The Council found that Lady Mary 'dyd use to have Masse sayd openly in her hows, refusing to have there celebrat the Servyce of the Communyon'. As politely as possible, they commanded that 'she would imbrase and cause to be celebrat in her saide howse the communion and other Devyne Services set forth by his Majestie'.

Throughout 1550, the Council intervened in a series of cases involving nobles and gentry covertly saying or singing Masses in their private houses. It was in reaction to such failure to conform that in 1552 the second Edwardian Act of Uniformity complained:

> A great number of people in divers parts of this realm, following their own sensuality, and living without knowledge or due fear of God, do wilfully and damnably…abstain and refuse to come to their parish churches.

As well as these individual misdemeanours, omissions, and refusals to conform, there were more dramatic, collective, and violent demonstrations of popular resistance to uniformity. These have come to be known as the Prayer Book Rebellions (described in Chapter 1). While the causes were also economic, Cranmer was certainly convinced of the confessional bias of the Devon and Cornwall rebels. He replied contemptuously to the Articles drawn up by the rebels and condemned in wholesale terms the ignorance of the Devonshire and Cornwall men. Their antipathy to modern doctrine he put down to sin and the devil. How could such a far-flung part of the country be expected to be educated and sophisticated enough to understand the new theology?

Ceremony and controversy

The enforcement became more clear in 1552, in the revised edition. Increasingly, the cause of controversy lay not so much in the words of the prayers that were said, as in the rubrics that prescribed how they were to be performed. Already in 1549 Cranmer included the special note 'Of Ceremonies', which showed how the ritual was political:

> And in these all our dooynges wee condemne no other nacions, nor prescribe anye thyng, but to oure owne people onelye. For we thinke it conveniente that every countreye should use such ceremonies, as thei shal thynke beste to the settyng foorth of goddes honor, and glorye: and to the reducyng of the people to a moste perfecte and Godly living, without errour or supersticion.

This is the only reference to 'nacion' in any edition of the *Book of Common Prayer* until 1662. It shows the ambition and the caution at the same time of the Reformed ritual.

With a nod to tradition, the 1549 Holy Communion provided that a priest wear 'a vestement or Cope' over his 'albe' (Box 8). This was soon tested by John Hooper (d.1555), exiled in Switzerland

Box 8 Vestments

Vestment is the term used for the special clothing worn during Christian services. The *alb* is a plain, ankle-length tunic with long sleeves. The word *alb* is short for the Latin phrase *tunica alba*, which means 'white tunic'; its origin was the staple clothing of the Roman Empire (Jesus is described as wearing one at the crucifixion).

Adapted for church use in the medieval church, it was traditionally made of white or undyed fabric. A priest wore it with a *stole*, a long, narrow rectangular garment worn around the neck so that it hangs down in front of the legs, ending below the knees. In the Eucharist, it was accompanied by the *chasuble*, a circular garment with a hole in the centre for the head. It was often decorated, as the celebrant wore it at Mass, over the *alb* and *stole*. The *cope* was an ornate cape-like garment worn in processions; cathedrals possessed different *copes* for different festivals in the church year, often described in elaborate detail in inventories.

At the Reformation, vestments became controversial among Lutherans, though many German churches retained them; other Reformed churches adopted a simple black *gown* or robe. In England, the alb could be exchanged for a *surplice*, a lightweight blouse-like garment with sleeves; it was worn over a *cassock*, a plain, lightweight, ankle-length garment with no hood, often black.

under Henry VIII. In February 1550, he refused the see of Gloucester to avoid wearing vestments. By contravening the Act of Uniformity this was a crime against the king. To resolve the issue, he debated with Ridley, Bishop of London. Hooper argued that vestments were not scriptural. Ridley disputed his interpretation and contended that this was an issue of authority in the church. He pointed out that adherence to the *Book of Common Prayer* now constituted the sole religious law in England.

Bucer recommended to Cranmer abolishing vestments, because they encouraged superstition; but ceased to support Hooper. Calvin wrote to Hooper agreeing the point of principle but advising that it was not worth such dangerous resistance. Having been sent to Fleet Prison, Hooper caved in and was consecrated Bishop of Gloucester on 8 March 1551, preaching before the king wearing vestments shortly after. Meanwhile, the 1552 *Book of Common Prayer* quietly omitted the vestments rubrics that had occasioned the controversy.

Over the next five years, Hooper, Ridley, and Cranmer were all burned at the stake under Mary I. Yet the legacy of their debates did not die with them. Among the survivors, some spent the years of wilderness in Geneva, where there were no vestments at all. Others, who stayed in England (like Matthew Parker (1504–75) the new Archbishop of Canterbury), accepted their use.

If at first it was in doubt what kind of religion Elizabeth would espouse, the *Book of Common Prayer* was reinstituted in 1559 almost entirely in line with 1552. An obscure rubric prefixed to Morning Prayer restored the vestments in use in 'the second year of the reign' of Edward. This rule remained even after 1662, although hardly anyone by then understood the reference to 1549. A copy in Corpus Christi College, Oxford bears the signatures of the Privy Council setting the price. Printing was placed in the hands of the Queen's Printers, a monopoly which marked the political status of the book for the whole of the next century and a half of religious conflict. Even to this day, only the university presses of Oxford and Cambridge are granted special permission to print the book outside official regulation.

In 1563, an attempt to revise the *Book of Common Prayer* on anti-vestiarian lines was defeated in Convocation, by a single vote. Parker moved against non-conformists, centring on the diocese of London, where the bishop, Edmund Grindal (*c.*1519–83), had favoured former exiles. In 1566, London clergy assembled at Lambeth Palace were ordered to wear square cap, gown, and surplice, and that they 'inviolably observe the rubric of the Book of Common Prayer, and the Queen majesty's injunctions'. They had to commit on the spot, in writing, yes or no. Sixty-one subscribed; thirty-seven did not, and were immediately suspended.

The result was widespread protest and a literary war. The tract *A Briefe Discourse Against the Outwarde Apparel of the Popishe Church* (1566) has been called 'the first Puritan manifesto'. From now on, there was an alternative wing in English Protestantism. In 1572, Thomas Wilcox and John Field published an *Admonition to Parliament*. Looking to Geneva for a model of church government, their argument now openly embraced separatism and the possibility of abolishing the episcopacy.

This may go some way to explain a radical shift in the perception of the *Book of Common Prayer* even while the text remained the same. From being the radical rallying point of 1552, its advocacy increasingly marked out the conformist and conservative Reformed position. In 1580/1 Robert Browne (d.1633) and Robert Harrison (d.1585?) formed the first separatist congregation at Norwich. Browne had attended Cambridge University, and was influenced by Thomas Cartwright (1534–1603), whose principal enemy was John Whitgift (*c.*1530–1604). Whitgift's rise in 1583 to become Archbishop of Canterbury marked the triumph of conformity. Although Whitgift often took Calvinist positions in theology, such as predestination, he had a horror of non-conformism of any kind, increasingly rooting out any signs either of Presbyterianism, or Catholic recusancy.

Orthodoxy for Whitgift meant the *Book of Common Prayer*, which was entirely predicated on the priesthood as a sacred office, needing its own ritual (in the Ordinal) to ordain priests and consecrate bishops. This included several elements borrowed from the ritual ordination of the Middle Ages: the laying on of hands; and the singing of an ancient hymn *Veni creator spiritus* ('Come holy ghost'). In 1550 every priest was also formally given a chalice, although this was removed in 1552 and replaced with a Bible.

For Puritans this was too much, and they pinned their hopes on an alternative. In Scotland, Knox introduced in 1559 the *Forme of Prayers*, based on Calvin's *La Forme des Prières*. It became known as *The Book of Common Order*, approved by the Scottish Assembly in 1564. By 1567 it was being used secretly in London. In 1585 a revised Genevan form was printed in London as *A Book of the Form of Common Prayers*, accompanying a bill in the House of Commons proposing it replace the *Book of Common Prayer*. Elizabeth I suppressed it, and its supporters were imprisoned in the Tower.

Protestants had to choose or make do. The Genevan or 'Breeches' Bible of 1560 provided Calvinist notes and catechisms, but was often bound with a copy of the *Book of Common Prayer* after 1583. Confessional conformity was now passing from church into private readership. In Shakespeare's *The Merchant of Venice* (2.2.144), Gratiano apologizes for not having his prayer book in his pocket. The remark reflects new book formats, with smaller sizes making copies portable. A quarto edition was first made in 1549, an octavo in 1552. The first sextodecimo was in 1570, and became more popular in the 1590s. The smallest of all, a 64° in 1600, is so tiny that it must demonstrate a trend towards using books as items of devotion. Even small copies often have births and deaths in the family inscribed in them.

From Communion rails to religious war

In 1603, as James Stuart entered London to claim his new throne, up to 1,000 Puritan ministers proposed the 'Millenary Petition'. Seeing that James had ruled over a Presbyterian country for much of his life, they hoped for reform of church discipline and liturgy in England. Among the complaints were questions of ritual: signing of the cross in baptism; the use of a ring in weddings; bowing at the name of Jesus; and requiring clergy to wear the surplice. In the event, at the Hampton Court Conference in 1604, James disappointed them. While approving a new translation of the Bible, he retained bishops and prayer book as epitomes of English national religion.

Jacobean piety at an official level began to lean towards liturgical traditionalism. Lancelot Andrewes (1555–1626), one of James's favourite bishops, emphasized reverence in worship, especially in Communion. This was a paradox of the English Reformation. The *Book of Common Prayer* enjoined weekly Holy Communion. George Herbert (1593–1633), courtier turned country parson, structured his book of devotional poems, *The Temple*, around the liturgy. This included 'Altar', 'Church-monuments', 'Mattens', 'Even-song'; and also several Eucharistic poems ('The H. Communion', 'The Banquett', 'Love (III)'). Yet he admitted that while administering Communion monthly was preferable, six times a year was more realistic.

If frequency was a problem, ceremony became central. In 1617, Francis Burgoyne, prebendary at Durham Cathedral, moved the Communion table back to the altar. William Laud (1573–1645), Dean of Gloucester, took a similar decision in the same year. This brought Laud into conflict with his Calvinist Bishop, Miles Smith. Twenty years later, Burgoyne's action in Durham still caused contention. Interestingly, the argument used by Peter Smart was that Burgoyne had altered things 'from the ould manner of standing which it had kept in all bishops times from the beginning of Queen Elizabeths raigne'. Far from restoring tradition, he had destroyed it: Smart, without exaggeration, called it 'spiritual fornication'. Laud, meanwhile, justified his actions on the grounds of cathedral practice elsewhere. Smart and Laud protested too much. Nobody knew where the altars had been, only where they should be, either at the east end, or in the nave, positions at devotional extremes.

Just as controversial was what to do in front of the altar, wherever it was. Complaints against ceremonialists included that they would 'ducke' and 'cringe', as they entered or departed the church, or on approaching the Communion table. In the 1630s, visitations enquired in an opposite direction whether bowing was enforced, though no Church Canon required it, and the *Book of Common Prayer* never mentioned it. Jeremy Taylor (d.1667) argued that the Communion table was equivalent to the Jewish holy of holies or 'Christ's mercy seat'. Reverence to the altar was only proper, the 'place of greatest sanctity' requiring 'the expression of the greatest devotion'. William Prynne (1600–69) in 1636–7 called such reverence idolatry and the 'will-worship of mans invention'. Laudians retorted that adoration *before* the altar was not the same as adoration *to* it.

Laudianism is the name given to this distinctive religious practice. Once Laud became Archbishop of Canterbury in 1633, he took it upon himself to make conformity in church furniture and human gesture paramount. Not only was the altar to be at the east wall, it was to be furnished with a rail, so that the congregation could kneel before the altar both for the consecration and to receive Communion. Sometimes the rails were ornately carved. Matthew Wren (1585–1667), a former chaplain of Andrewes, rebuilt the chapel at Peterhouse, Cambridge, combining the Baroque with a form of early Gothic revival, including stained glass windows.

For Laud, ceremonies are neither ornamental nor merely external, but a means of expressing 'the beauty of holiness'. But Laudianism also had a theological and political edge. Andrewes, as Dean of the Chapel Royal, instructed the new King Charles I in anti-Calvinist theology opposed to predestination, and Charles combined this with emotional attachment to vestments and ornament. The Arminians (named after the distinguished Dutch anti-Calvinist divine, Jacobus Arminius) were identified both as political faction and doctrinal camp: 'What do the Arminians hold?' it was asked; 'All the best deaneries and bishoprics'. This was a piquant feature of anti-Laudian polemic. As the divisions of the 1630s widened into the Civil War of 1642, the *Book of Common Prayer* had become a badge of the royalist party, with church ceremonies its cultural clothing, as much as cavalier hats and lace.

In 1637, Prynne had his ears cut off for writing pamphlets against Laud, and Elizabethan statutes were revived, fining those who refused to attend Church of England services. Meanwhile in Scotland, Charles I attempted to enforce for the first time a special edition of the *Book of Common Prayer* printed in Edinburgh. According to legend, Jenny Geddes, a street seller, threw a stool at the minister in St Giles's Kirk, crying out 'daur ye say Mass in my lug?' ('dare you say mass in my ear?'). A riot broke out and rebellion followed in other cities: Figure 4 shows the commotion in St Andrews when the prelate tried to use the Scottish Prayer Book. To suppress the rebellion, Charles had to call a new Parliament in England in November 1640 to raise money.

The Root and Branch Petition of 1640—signed by 15,000 Londoners and presented to Parliament a year later by Oliver Cromwell (1599–1658) and Sir Henry Vane the Younger (1613–62)—called for the elimination of episcopacy, 'root and branch', and singled out the *Book of Common Prayer* for opprobrium: the 'Liturgy for the most part is framed out of the Romish Breviary, Rituals and Mass-Book'.

In the lead-up to the Civil Wars, Puritans hated signing with the cross during baptism above all else. 'It is the mark of the beast',

4. A riot over the *Book of Common Prayer* in St Andrews, Scotland, 1637; John Vicars, *A sight of y[e] trans-actions of these latter yeares emblemized with ingraven plats, which men may read without spectacles* ([London]: Are to be sould, by Thomas Ienner, in his shop at the old Exchange, [1646]), sig. A4[r].

an Essex man declared; incidents in that county record a child being snatched from the priest's hands; or the face being covered by a cloth; or even the curate's hand being twisted behind his back, to prevent the ritual taking place. The sect known as Fifth Monarchists, especially widespread in the New Model Army, favoured adult baptism, by full immersion. Ritual was on the run.

In 1645 Laud was executed, and the *Book of Common Prayer* was abolished the same year. For fifteen years in the 17th century, as under Mary I for five years in the 16th century—but for opposite theological reasons—the *Book of Common Prayer* disappeared from view. A new book, *A Directory for the Public Worship of God*, was published in its place, much more in line with continental Protestantism. Some clandestine use of the *Book of Common Prayer* continued, although usually in abridged form. John Evelyn (1620–1706) in his diary reports celebrating prayer book

Communion at home at Christmas in 1657, only to be interrupted by soldiers. Meanwhile clergymen such as Jeremy Taylor experimented with newly discovered ancient liturgies to create new English forms. In exile, royalists such as Evelyn and Cosin worshipped in Paris using the old book, praying for its return.

Restoring the religious nation

On 29 May 1660, the king's birthday, Charles II re-entered London after eleven years of exile, in a festival that lasted three days. Bonfires burned in Melton Mowbray for three days and nights. If the 1662 edition sounds as inevitable as the Restoration itself, little is as it seems. Before his return to England, a deputation of ministers requested that Charles abstain from using the *Book of Common Prayer* in his private chapel. In the Declaration of Breda, signed in the Netherlands in April 1660, Charles recognized that 'the passion and uncharitableness of the times have produced several opinions in religion, by which men are engaged in parties and animosities against each other', and promised 'a liberty to tender consciences' in his new regime. The Presbyterians, by no means few in number, were especially tender about the old prayer book, which they considered to contain 'many things that are justly offensive and need amendment'. They repeated complaints well known since the Millenary Petition of 1603.

If some were looking for a resurrection of the *Book of Common Prayer*, others came not to praise the book but to bury it. To many, the book appeared to be a thing of the past. The revolution that did away with the monarch in 1649 had removed bishops, deans, and cathedral chapters. The festivals of the church calendar were banned, including, notoriously, Christmas Day; the buildings of former cathedrals were vandalized and left as dilapidated symbols of lost ecclesiastical power. At Lichfield the roof had fallen in; Canterbury was a carcass of stone; Durham was used as a prison, St Paul's as a stable and shopping mall, St Asaph as a wine shop.

A fifth of clergy had been deprived of livings; the bishops quietly retired, and when they died they were not replaced.

How far practice on the ground reflected parliamentary ordinance is a matter of conjecture. One study of churchwardens' accounts of the late 1640s shows the illegal *Book of Common Prayer* present in a third of churches examined; and less than a quarter owning the new *Directory*. Whether this reflects local feeling or instead a time-honoured reluctance of churches to spend money on new books is less easy to assess. However, the sense that it was a book on the way out and barely being kept alive is found not only among radical Protestants but among its most sacramentalist defenders. Wren, locked up in the Tower, remarked that there had never been a better opportunity to amend the errors in the old prayer book, since 'it hath been so long disused that not one of five hundred is so perfect in it as to observe alterations'.

The new edition of 1662 is thus not an act of acclamation so much as one of conscious cultural retrieval. The restored monarchy claimed merely to be setting the clocks back, undoing the unfortunate interlude and carrying on as normal. But in some ways it was as consciously revolutionary as anything seen in the fifteen-year radical interval. Part of this new revolution was a deliberate ideology of memory. The wonderfully entitled 'Act of Oblivion' of May 1660, or 'An Act of Free and General Pardon, Indemnity, and Oblivion' to give its full title, is a masterpiece of euphemism and culturally encoded commemoration and noisy forgetting. Who was being remembered and who forgotten? Disappointed Royalists, it is said, commented that the Act meant 'indemnity for [the king's] enemies and oblivion for his friends'. Oblivion meant contradictory things at the same time. The regicides were punished in the most outrageous way possible. At the same time the new regime was involved in countless small acts of what psychologists now call 'false memory'. Nostalgia for things Caroline meant what nostalgia always brings: fabrication of a past that never was, or that was too good to be true.

Charles put his own feelings on the table in the Worcester Declaration of October 1660:

> we do esteem the Liturgy of the Church of England, contained in the Book of Common Prayer, and by law established, to be the best we have seen; and we believe that we have seen all that are extant and used in this part of the world.

The Savoy Conference followed. The warrant was issued on 25 March 1661, even-handedness on magnificent display. Twelve bishops were appointed, along with twelve Presbyterian divines. The bishops included Cosin, newly Bishop of Durham, a student of liturgical history for decades, and John Gauden (1605–62), the reputed author of *Eikon Basilike*, a royalist tract which claimed Charles I as a martyr. The Presbyterians included Richard Baxter (1615–91), armed with a full plan for a new reformed liturgy.

Both sides imagined they were getting a better bargain than was the case. The Presbyterians thought they had gained the upper hand by having revision discussed at all. Yet it soon became clear that the base standard for discussion was the existing *Book of Common Prayer*, and any hopes to negotiate it away were already gone. On the other hand, those on the episcopal side who thought that they had carte blanche to reverse the tide of Puritanism and return the *Book of Common Prayer* to a more serious ritual engagement with the past, were also disappointed. The object of the Savoy Conference was scrupulously to satisfy neither party, even to leave well alone. The 1662 revision can be seen as a triumph for announcing large-scale revision while keeping things the same. Yet it is in this achievement of restoring the book at all that 1662 was in its way radical.

The complexity of the Presbyterian position can be ascertained via its leader, Baxter. He had been ordained deacon in 1638. In Shropshire before the Civil War he considered the *Book of Common Prayer* lawful, although he found 'much *disorder* and *defectiveness* in it'. But when he encountered religious radicalism at close quarters in the New Model Army in 1645 he was equally disconcerted.

Acting as an army chaplain, he endorsed the principle of baptism and rejected the antinomian belief in the exclusive exercise of free grace characteristic of the Ranters. His 1649 publication, *Aphorismes of Justification*, argued against strict predestination and incorporated human cooperation with grace, leading to accusations of Arminianism, popery, and even Pelagianism.

It was during the 1650s, under the Commonwealth, that Baxter achieved national prominence as a result of his ministry at Kidderminster. Here he attempted a middle way between radical Puritanism and prayer book worship. He tolerated written liturgy but used extemporary prayers; he advised communicants to remain seated during the sacrament, but did not refuse to administer it to those who knelt. He did not observe Christmas but he liked church music; 'God would not have given us, either our Senses themselves, or their usual objects, if they might not have been serviceable to his own praise', he said.

If Baxter does not conform to the Puritan cliché, something similar can be said about conformist bishops on the other side, even their champion, Cosin. He was associated with Laudianism from 1623, when he became chaplain to Richard Neile (1562–1640), Bishop of Durham. At Peterhouse in Cambridge, where he was master in the 1630s, he gave full expression to ceremonies both in matter and in spirit: he installed a new altar at the east end, with crucifix and candlesticks; and encouraged signing with the cross, kissing the book, and bowing at the name of Jesus.

If the Commonwealth brought fame to Baxter, to Cosin came exile. If his opponents imagined him only too happy in Catholic Paris, he himself found his new hosts 'exceeding uncharitable and somewhat worse' in their exercise of religion. He compared them unfavourably with the Geneva camp (a serious insult for Cosin) for threatening damnation on anyone who did not accept their articles of faith. He disliked the way his companions and servants were proselytized, and it caused him great personal distress when his son defected to Catholicism in 1652.

In Paris he became more Protestant, even while maintaining his prayer book beliefs. Crucially, on the Eucharist, while ratifying his belief in real presence, he argued that the 'body and blood are neither sensibly present'. Their benefit is limited to those 'prepared to receive them', and only in the act of receiving. This is intriguingly close to Cranmer's mature position, influencing Cosin's minute attention to the question of what to do with leftover consecrated bread in the 1662 text, a strikingly ambiguous lacuna in 1552.

The 1662 *Book of Common Prayer*

The Savoy Conference began on Easter Monday, 15 April 1661, and ended on 25 July. The Bishop of London, Gilbert Sheldon (1598–1677), like any good chair of a committee, made a brilliant initial point of procedure. The conference convened, he said, at the request of the Presbyterians, and thus they should begin by making a list of complaints and suggestions. The bishops, he moved, had nothing to do until the Presbyterian case was presented. So subtle was this, the Presbyterians agreed. They thereby showed their hand entire. As a result they were cast as innovators (in a negative sense); the conference proceeded through their objections, one by one, arguing them down.

The Presbyterians produced the so-called *Exceptions* on 4 May. This consists of eighteen larger points and many pages of detail. The preface argues, not unreasonably, that the work was over a hundred years old, and had been written for different times. It was too close to the Roman rite. This vein is continued in Article III, which complains about 'the repetitions, and responsals of the clerk and people, and the alternate reading of the psalms and hymns'. This produces 'a confused murmur' in the church, as each side is confused as to who should say what; unspoken is a Puritan antipathy to formality of prayer and ritual, and a desire to free up 'the gift of prayer' (especially longer formats), allowing improvised petitioning of God for daily needs.

Other articles address four different kinds of traditional Puritan complaint: the observance of holy days; too much ceremonial, bordering on superstition; an objection to absolution, and a resistance to assuming the whole of the congregation is regenerate and destined for heaven; and lastly, a plea for clarity of language and expression (appealing again to an idea that the book was outdated). One of the main pleas here is for the King James translation to replace the Great Bible text, which had not been changed since 1549, even by James.

As well as general points, the Presbyterians produced seventy-eight objections to particulars, again including points of doctrine, ceremony, and defects in wording: an example of the last is the use of the word 'worship' in the marriage vows, no longer felt as idiomatic. Sheldon's cunning became evident when the *Answer to the Exceptions* emerged a month later. He forbade general discussion from first principles. The bishops appealed to common order. This is subtly joined to a dismissal of extemporary prayer: 'great care may be taken to suppress those private conceptions of prayers before and after sermon, lest private opinions be made the matter of prayer in public'. Responsals are justified precisely in contrast to Puritan fondness for long prayers: they work 'by quickening, continuing, and uniting our devotion, which is apt to freeze or sleep, or flat in a long continued prayer or form'. A waspish side note describes the 'long tedious prayer' of non-conformists as continually interrupted by loud 'Amens' from Puritan congregations: 'mutual exultations, provocations, petitions, holy contentions and strivings'. These are as much a way of showing off their own piety as stirring up the zeal of others.

In conclusion, the bishops made seventeen bullet-point concessions, including the use of the King James Bible, something they wanted in any case. Even so, Coverdale's translation remained in the Psalter, perhaps because of long habit in singing. The bishops' agreement was faint to the point of derisory. They allowed the words 'with my body I thee worship' to be changed to 'with my body I thee honour'; but this never appeared in the eventual 1662 *Book of Common Prayer*.

The doom of the Presbyterians lay not only in the new text, but in the exclusion from ministry of any who did not swear to its uniformity. Baxter foresaw this clearly. Yet we should not take defeat of the Presbyterian party as an overwhelming victory for Episcopalians. Traditionalists had wanted their own revisions to the book as it had come down in its 1559 and 1604 forms. Wren, Bishop of Ely, spent eighteen years in the Tower wrestling with every word. Cosin saw Wren's *Advices* after returning from Paris in 1660. He combined his researches with Wren's in compiling the 'Durham Book', a 1619 prayer book which Cosin drenched in his own ink.

Closest to Cosin's heart was the form of Communion. As early as 1628 in his *Collection of Private Devotions*, he had reprinted part of the Canon from 1549 as a private prayer to be said at consecration. A 'back to 1549' movement became the Laudian dream. In annotating the Durham Book, Cosin came across a solution he had not seen before. In the 1637 Scottish *Book of Common Prayer*, James Wedderburn reintroduced the *epiclesis* (the calling of the Holy Spirit into the elements) from the 1549 Canon; restored the Prayer of Oblation to its original function; and excised what he called a 'Zwinglian tenet' from the 1552 sentences, that the sacrament is a bare sign of remembrance. Cosin made full use of the Scottish book (while never mentioning it) as well as 1549 in the Durham Book, finding plenty of room for Laudian furniture and vestment.

Sheldon's politics outmanoeuvred Cosin as well as Baxter. Neither Sheldon nor the Earl of Clarendon was much of a ritualist. Both were realists, who knew the 1549 Canon spelt trouble. It did not even reach discussion: Sheldon's whole object was to restore the book in use in 1642, in effect 1552. Nevertheless, the Durham Book was the practical starting point for the revised book of 1662, which now began in earnest. William Sancroft (1617–93), Cosin's chaplain, incorporated some of Wren's and Cosin's earlier work in improving the rubrics in about eighty places, and the spoken text in sixty-six.

In November 1661 Convocation passed (after sixteen hours' sitting) every jot and tittle of the new book. In all, 4,500 words were removed and 10,500 added. The 1662 edition was full of small improvements, as well as the containment of controversial points. The rubrics were altered in many places with greater clarity; the Collects were embellished; the service for burial, in a version written by Robert Sanderson (1587–1663), has greater dignity and pathos than 1552.

Yet 1662 is in substance close to 1552. It is more an old book than a new one. Fittingly, perhaps, the most famous of its novelties, 'A General Thanksgiving', was composed by Edward Reynolds (1599–1676), a Presbyterian representative at Savoy, though also a bishop. Reynolds led the moderate Presbyterians through the 1650s, but did not conform to a stereotype of the Civil War non-conformist. He was learned in Greek literature, and wrote a *Treatise on the Passions*. It is in the spirit of that work that Reynolds provides an emotional register for Christian worship (Box 9).

The sentiment owes much to the Puritans, and the 'General Thanksgiving' as a whole is the nearest thing in the *Book of Common Prayer* to the kind of long prayer the Presbyterians wanted to see throughout. By a delicious irony, which would not have been lost on Reynolds, it is now the prayer most beloved of *Book of Common Prayer* traditionalists.

Box 9 The General Thanksgiving of 1662

God, Father of all mercies, we thine unworthy servants do give thee most humble and hearty thanks for all thy goodness and loving kindness to us, and to all men; We bless thee for our creation, preservation, and all the blessings of this life, but above all for thine inestimable love in the redemption of the world by our Lord Jesus Christ; for the means of grace, and for the hope of glory. And we beseech thee give us that due sense of all thy mercies, that our hearts may be unfeignedly thankful, and that we shew forth thy praise, not only with our lips, but in our lives, by giving up ourselves to thy service, and by walking before thee in holiness and righteousness all our days, through Jesus Christ our Lord, to whom with thee and the holy Ghost be all honour and glory, world without end. *Amen.* (OWC, 268)

Nevertheless, the first consequence of the Act of Uniformity in 1662, as in 1549, was exclusion. Over 2,000 clergy were expelled from the Church of England for refusing to swear to the new book. This became known as the 'Great Ejection'. They included Baxter. For thirty years, this model moderate was persecuted and periodically imprisoned. Yet he continued to advocate a national church, off and on, until his death in 1691. From now on, non-conformity became enshrined in British social life, as Methodists, Baptists, Quakers, and other groups struggled against established religion. By law, a substantial section of society was excluded from public affairs for a century and a half, Catholics and Protestants alike, for the sake of their religion, and in the name of common prayer.

Chapter 5
Empire and prayer book

Shipwrecked off the Atlantic coast of South America, Robinson Crusoe delves into the sinking vessel in order to retrieve some essentials for survival. There, he finds treasure, including rum, cheese, biscuits, and sugar; pistols, swords, gunpowder, and an axe; a hammock, a spade, a pair of scissors, and a pen with ink; and finally, some writings: navigational charts, three English Bibles, and 'two or three Popish prayer-books'. This last may be Daniel Defoe's idea of a dissenter's joke. His parents were Presbyterian dissenters, and he was taught by Charles Morton, a leading non-conformist, at a school in Newington Green outside London.

In creating the eponymous protagonist of *Robinson Crusoe* in 1719, Defoe (*c*.1660–1731) endows his philosophical autodidact with an exemplary education on a blank canvas. 'I had hitherto acted upon no Religious Foundation at all, indeed I had very few notions of Religion in my Head', Robinson reflects. Fortune has brought him to the island, he believes, until the mysterious appearance of barley, in soil not accustomed to it, suggests to him the intervention of divine providence. Soon, the appearance of a flaming angel in a dream brings him to a calamitous repentance and a kind of conversion. 'Lord be my Help, for I am in great Distress', Robinson cries: the first prayer, he says, 'that I had made for many years'.

Irony is never far away in Defoe. The barley, Robinson realizes later, comes from the chance survival of seeds from the ship. His prayers, too, do not come from nowhere. Before his conversion, when he hears an earthquake, he utters a first premonition of religious feeling, 'Lord ha' Mercy upon me'. It is a citation straight out of the *Book of Common Prayer*, in its revised 1662 version, from the *Te Deum* in Morning Prayer. Defoe makes prayer book religion seem the most tenuous form of faith, the barest seed to which providence may stretch a helping hand. Yet even when Robinson ascends to a more serious contemplation of his sinful nature and his need for redemption, his prayers sound not unlike the familiar forms of the English Litany, by way of Psalm 107:

> That it may please thee to succour, help, and comfort, all that are in danger, necessity, and tribulation;
> *We beseech thee to hear us, good Lord.* (OWC, 262)

Defoe may be laughing behind his back here at the *Book of Common Prayer*, rejected by his teacher and his parents, as the definition of rote-learned and unenthusiastic religion. True repentance needs to be felt personally, and true prayer is from the heart. Robinson is a reluctant convert at best. Yet in creating the innocent mind of the pre-religious Robinson, Defoe simultaneously gives voice to the universal concerns of nascent colonial consciousness: how to imbue the native mind with peculiarly English godliness.

God's English in the British Isles

The words 'to propagate the worship of God in the English tongue' became in time the motto of the British Empire in the 19th century. Their first appearance, however, is nearly as old as the *Book of Common Prayer* itself, in a proclamation accompanying the first edition made outside of England.

In 1551, Humphrey Powell, granted £20 sterling by the Privy Council towards the costs of setting up as royal printer in Dublin, issued *The Booke of Common Praier*, the earliest book printed with moveable type in Ireland. It was first used on Easter Sunday, 1551, at Christ Church Cathedral, Dublin. At the end of the book there is inserted a special prayer for the Lord Deputy of Ireland, to be said between the two last Collects of the Litany. This prayer for Sir James Croft (d.1590), mentioned by name, became the first prayer for a commoner in the *Book of Common Prayer*'s history. As well as assistance in the administration of justice, the prayer begs divine help for Croft in delivering 'rest, peace and quietnesse' in place of the 'accustomed, most frowarde and divelishe sedicions' of the Irish.

The new religious book is thus explicitly one of conquest as well as conversion. The order of Edward VI also required the services to be translated into Irish 'in those places which need it'. There is a threat here of linguistic control. Indeed, the prior intention was that Irish ministry should be English speaking. Only if an English speaker could not be found was an Irish speaker permitted. The Tudor government in Ireland thus used English religion as a means of anglicization as well as colonization. No translation of the liturgy into Irish (the language of the vast majority of the population) was made until 1608. The translator, William Daniel (Huilliam O'Domhnuill, d.1628), consecrated Archbishop of Tuam in 1609, previously helped make an Irish New Testament. In the preface Daniel wrote (in English) that the aim of translation was 'that the ignorant may understand, how grosely they are abused by their blind malitious guides, which beare them in hand that our divine service is nothing else, but the service of the Devil'. However, in a country notably resistant to English, the 1560 Latin translation of the book was often preferred, as indeed also in the colleges of Oxford and Cambridge.

Anti-Catholicism is the natural colonial dialect of the English in Ireland, but the book also made some controversial compromises, including prayers for St Patrick's Day. An early surviving copy in York Minster Library includes annotations from the Latin Vulgate Bible, along with trenchant Gaelic political verses. Religious colonization proved vexatious. In a survey of 224 parishes in 1576, only eighteen curates knew English. In contrast, the effect of the new policy was that by 1604 only three rectors knew Irish. This was nonsensical in relation to a supposed aspiration to win over congregations 'beyond the Pale' (the area immediately around Dublin where English settlers congregated). Outside Dublin, Irish was the prevailing language.

In other Celtic areas of the British Isles, vernaculars were tolerated in proportion to religious political affiliation. In recusant Cornwall, imposing the English language went hand in hand with imposing Protestant religion, a process repeated in the Isle of Man. In Wales, by contrast, the Tudors were hailed as Welsh, and the gentry backed union. Already in 1549 John Oswen was given a licence to publish the *Book of Common Prayer* in Worcester for use in the Welsh borders. In 1563 Parliament ordered that the New Testament and *Book of Common Prayer* be translated into Welsh. The translations were undertaken by Richard Davies, Bishop of St David's (d.1581), and William Salesbury (d.1584?), first appearing in 1567. The Welsh-language enthusiast Salesbury was a partisan for a Reformed Church of England.

A French translation of the *Book of Common Prayer* was prepared for use in Calais and the Channel Islands in 1553, but not widely used. Spanish, Portuguese, and Greek translations of the *Book of Common Prayer* were used rather as propaganda for the authenticity of the Church of England. In Italy, this combined in the Napoleonic period with a bizarrely futile effort of national conversion, beginning with the Waldensian community in the alpine valleys of Piedmont. The Waldensians happily took financial support but ignored the English liturgy.

Other early translations attempted to control the worship of Protestant refugee immigrants in England, often the result of exile. A French version was made for the Walloon Church in Norwich in 1616. Archbishop Laud viewed the self-governing Dutch and French émigré congregations in London as 'great nurseries of inconformity'. He investigated how many of their members had been born in England, and how many attended their local parish church. On 19 December 1634, an order was issued for all English-born members of foreign churches to attend services at their parish churches; non-natives should use the English liturgy in translation. However, a Dutch translation of the *Book of Common Prayer* was not issued until 1645, the year of Laud's death.

These parallel linguistic and liturgical strategies continued in the 17th century. In 1662, the Act of Uniformity ordered the bishops of Hereford, St David's, St Asaph, Bangor, and Llandaff to ensure that the *Book of Common Prayer* 'be truly and exactly Translated into the *British* or *Welsh* tongue' (OWC, 205) and printed in enough numbers for every 'Cathedral, Collegiate, and Parish-Church' in Wales.

In Ireland in the 1630s, the religious policy of Thomas Wentworth, Earl of Strafford (1593–1641), recognized that the church nominally had enormous resources, but many leases were secured by laymen at low long-term rents. In most parishes the endowment was insufficient to support an incumbent. Wentworth's priority was to re-endow churches by appointing bishops less for spiritual qualities than a capacity to raise funds. Plantation was the key to securing an Irish kingdom under the dominion of an imperial Crown: 'plantations must be the only means under God and your majesty to reform this subject as well in religion as in manners'. However, settlers (and outlaws) encouraged to seize farms in Ulster came mainly from the Scottish lowlands. They brought with them ministers who were

Calvinist in doctrine and inclined to a Presbyterian system of church government.

Indeed, Scotland remained immune to the *Book of Common Prayer*, even after the union of the kingdoms under James I and Charles I. As we saw in Chapter 4, the Scottish *Book of Common Prayer* in 1637 was a distant cause of the outbreak of Civil War in 1642. Rebellion in Ireland led to gleeful abolition of the hated *Book of Common Prayer*, but the restoration of Charles II brought reimposition in the Irish Act of Uniformity in 1665. The power of the book lasted to the Irish disestablishment of 1871 and beyond. Non-Anglicans were disbarred from political service, and the Irish intelligentsia saw Protestantism and English imperialism as synonymous.

The American prayer book: from colony to independence

The provision of regular worship was imposed in Virginia from its first settlement in 1607, and possession of the 1604 *Book of Common Prayer* was required of all clergy. Alexander Whitaker (1585–1617), minister between 1611 and his death, declared that 'every Sabbath we preach in the forenoon and catechize in the afternoon'. Once every month he said Communion, in which case he was more zealous than common practice in England in the same period.

The Jamestown chapel was sixty feet in length, and the Lord Governor repaired it some years later 'with a chancel of cedar and a communion table of black walnut. The font was hewn hollow like a canoe, and there were two bells in the steeple at the west end.' This rather idealistic description, with its mix of Laudian and evangelical forms of piety, conceals some of the difficulties of Virginian religion. Many of the ministers who arrived in America had been ordained in the Church of England but had emigrated because they were Puritan in leaning. In 1647, Governor Berkeley introduced a law declaring that ministers refusing to read Common Prayer were not entitled to receive tithes. This implies that ministers may have been using the *Directory for Public Worship* produced by the Commonwealth regime in England.

A dozen Anglican churches were established in Virginia by 1634 and another fifty by 1668. Despite a shortage of clergy, rudimentary instruction was afforded in many parishes by lay readers. There was a smaller number of Catholics and non-conformists. In Maryland, Catholics, Anglicans, Independents, Presbyterians, Anabaptists, and Quakers lived side by side. In New England, by contrast, where dissenters congregated in large numbers, there was no known Anglican minister in 1656. In the 1620s, early settlers in Massachusetts, migrating outwards from Plymouth, rejected separatism but argued that the Church of England should be reformed.

There were different motives for new settlements: early Rhode Islanders complained that the religious establishment in Massachusetts had imposed an intolerant hegemony; New Haven's founders thought that Massachusetts churches were insufficiently orthodox. Roger Williams (*c*.1606–83) called the Massachusetts church impure because it neither rejected the Church of England, nor instituted strict criteria to ensure its membership was not unregenerate.

By the early 18th century these patterns of religious practice were changing. A new charter in Massachusetts in 1691 guaranteed liberty of conscience for all Protestants; New England was no longer exclusively Puritan. While many of the 17th-century immigrants to Carolina had been dissenters from the Church of England, and Quakers dominated some of its Assemblies, in 1715 the Church of England was established in the two Carolinas. In 1710 Presbyterians were estimated as the largest group, but Anglicans only just behind.

In Virginia, the Church of England was seen as the perfect expression of colonial order. This was a means of social as much as spiritual control. In the mid-18th century, Sunday service began at eleven in the morning and consisted of Morning Prayer, the Litany, and the Ante-Communion from the *Book of Common Prayer*, with a moralizing sermon founded on a text from scripture. Weekly worship lasted around an hour and a half; in some localities this was supplemented with Evening Prayer; Holy Communion took place four times a year.

The case for seeing the Church of England as the bastion of colonial social order can be seen from the efforts of people such as Sir Edmund Andros (1637–1714), governor general of New England in the brief period of its conglomerate existence just before the Glorious Revolution. Shortly after his arrival in 1686, Andros asked each of the Puritan churches in Boston if its meeting house could be used for services of the Church of England. The royal instructions concerning religion in Virginia issued by the Privy Council in 1679 strove to ensure use of the *Book of Common Prayer*, with Holy Communion restricted to the proper rites of the established Church; clergymen should have a certificate from the Bishop of London. This brought attendant problems of cost in supplying the necessary copies of the *Book of Common Prayer*, as well as sufficient Communion plate. However, by the 18th century the problem of personnel had subsided: ministers increasingly had colonial origins rather than emigrating from England.

Church architecture also reflected the colonial world view. Virginian 18th-century churches favoured a simple brick building in cross formation. Pews imitated the hierarchy of local family standing. The pulpit, prominent in position, enforced the values of conformity and obedience. Attendance at public worship was significant, and absence brought murmurs of discontent from neighbours. The colonial gentry expected their ministers to conform to their needs in turn: in 1771, the wealthy landowner

Landon Carpenter asked the rector why he had not prayed for rain during a drought.

During the War of Independence, this conformity inevitably came into conflict when confronted with loyalty to the king. Ordination in the Church of England required an oath of allegiance. Many clergy after 1776 escaped to England or to Canada. However, conformist church governance did not lose its attractiveness in the new Republic. Unlike France, liberties in America were not intrinsically anti-clerical. In 1785, representatives of seven states met in Philadelphia to form a Protestant Episcopal Church of the United States of America. Among the proposals was a thorough-going revision of the *Book of Common Prayer*. Yet, as in England in 1662, drafting a new book acceptable to all parties proved extremely difficult. References to king and parliament were obviously eliminated. The monarch's birthday was replaced by a service to celebrate 'the inestimable Blessings of Religious and Civil Liberty; to be used yearly Fourth Day of July' (Box 10).

Evangelical Episcopalians in Connecticut, New Jersey, and New York, and in some southern states, wished to go further, removing the Nicene and Athanasian Creeds, or taking away the signing of the cross in baptism, along with the word 'regeneration'. The high church party in Virginia was not happy with this. Nor were the bishops in England who, in a strange act of non-independence, were newly consulted.

The General Convention of 1789 therefore accepted a compromise book. The Nicene Creed was restored, despite evangelical concerns about the clause in which Christ 'descended into hell'. In Holy Communion, however, there was an unexpected change: the restoration of the epiclesis, in which it is prayed that the bread and wine 'may become the body and blood of thy most dearly beloved son'. This was present in 1549 but had disappeared in 1552, replaced by a prayer for worthy reception: 'Grant that we...be partakers of his most blessed body and blood.' The reason

Box 10 Thanksgiving for 4 July, from the proposed American *Book of Common Prayer*, 1786

O God, whose Name is excellent in all the earth, and thy glory above the heavens, who as on this day didst inspire and direct the hearts of our delegates in Congress, to lay the perpetual foundations of peace, liberty, and safety; we bless and adore thy glorious Majesty, for this thy loving kindness and providence. And we humbly pray that the devout sense of this signal mercy may renew and increase in us a spirit of love and thankfulness to thee its only author, a spirit of peaceable submission to the laws and government of our country, and a spirit of fervent zeal for our holy religion, which thou hast preserved and secured to us and our posterity. May we improve these inestimable blessings for the advancement of religion, liberty, and science throughout this land, till the wilderness and solitary place be glad through us, and the desert rejoice and blossom as the rose. This we beg through the merits of Jesus Christ our Saviour. *Amen.*

was that the drafter of this section had been ordained in Scotland, where the 1755 version still followed the ill-fated text of the 1637 Scottish Prayer Book. A little piece of Laudianism thus passed over into the American spirit. By one of the many ironies of continuity embedded in the history of the *Book of Common Prayer*, even as the colonies were disbanded, the post-colonial influence of English religion continued to hold sway in the United States, down to modern times.

Empire, language, and mission

In 1787, another new version of the *Book of Common Prayer* in North America presents a very different picture of colonialism. It announces itself as a translation 'into the Mohawk Language' by Captain Joseph Brant (1743–1807). Brant, in fact, was both a full captain in the British Army, and an Iroquois chief otherwise known as 'Thayendanegea'. He had been instrumental in setting up the reserves in south-western Ontario known as the Six Nations of the Grand River. The engraving of the frontispiece (Figure 5) shows King George III presenting the *Book of Common Prayer* to the kneeling chief of the Mohawks; the chief's wife in turn kneels before Queen Charlotte. The king looks grateful that his Native American subjects have proved more loyal than the white colonials who joined the revolutionary army. Yet it also palpably demonstrates the ambiguous position which this legacy lay upon Brant and his followers in acting as an insurgent army against the rebel colonists. After the American victory, when the British ceded their claim to land, the Americans forced their allies (Mohawk and others) to give up their territories in New York. Most of the Mohawks migrated to Canada, where the Crown gave them a small parcel of land in compensation, in forts at Niagara, and another near Montreal.

The title of the book is nonetheless in Mohawk, still in the 21st century the most widely spoken of the dozen or so Northern Iroquoian languages. In linguistic terms, these languages are polysynthetic. In other words, a single Iroquoian word may contain as much information as a whole sentence in English. European documentation of the Iroquoian languages began in the mid-1530s with two short vocabularies. A Mohawk variant, however, first appears in print in Protestant catechisms designed to combat Jesuit missionary work.

In 1710 a small party of Christian Mohawks (led by 'King Hendrick') was brought to London by the Mayor of Albany to be presented to Queen Anne. At the same time, in reverse, a mission was sent to Fort Hunter by the Society for the Propagation of the Gospel in Foreign Parts, founded by Royal Charter in 1701 (later the SPG). The Society published Morning and Evening Prayer in New York in 1715. Included are segments from the *Book of Common Prayer*, selected psalms, the Book of Genesis, and the Gospel of St Matthew. Apart from section headings, it was entirely

FRONTISPIECE

5. Frontispiece by James Peachey showing King George III and Queen Charlotte receiving the homage of the Mohawks; from a Mohawk Book of Common Prayer: *Ne yakawea yondere anayendaghkwa oghseragwegouh* (London: C. Buckton, 1787).

in Mohawk. The 1787 Mohawk *Book of Common Prayer* contained three untranslated hymns: a 'Hymn on Repentance', 'Christening Hymn', and 'Burial Hymn'; it was produced in London and shipped back. In the same decade came two Mohawk Christian primers which began with the alphabet and then included prayers and catechisms. This was followed in the 19th century by Bibles produced by the British and Foreign Bible Society in London and Montreal, and by the American Bible Society in New York.

From the middle of the 19th century, the goal of the Church of England in the burgeoning empire switched from the needs of the colonial English to mission among non-English peoples. This entailed more than a change of language. The *Book of Common Prayer* took on the mantle of colonial acculturation. The official justification for this was Christian piety and the educational needs of indigenous peoples. However, in Canada, the Church Missionary Society (CMS) and the SPG struggled to learn unfamiliar and difficult languages. The missionary William Duncan (1832–1918) later complained that the *Book of Common Prayer* inhibited understanding, recommending simpler approaches to prayer and preaching that abandoned clerical hierarchy, formality, and authoritative printed texts. Duncan, however, was a rarity, and elsewhere ritual quickly became a code for native obedience and uniformity of cultural order.

The Cape of Good Hope in southern Africa, on the sea route between Europe and the East, was under Dutch control, and in 1749 the first service using the *Book of Common Prayer* was conducted in a Dutch Reformed Church. Even after the Cape was ceded to the British in 1814, most of the European population was Dutch. There was no Anglican bishop, and confirmations could not take place except when a new Bishop of Calcutta was appointed and stopped over en route to India. Only in 1848 did Robert Gray (1809–72) become Bishop of Cape Town, followed in 1870 by the foundation of a full province of the Church of South Africa.

Early experiment in worship among the Zulu in the 1870s was extravagantly ritualistic. In Natal, mission churches used an altar cross and lighted candles. Converts were baptized in open rivers accompanied by a Eucharist with a full choir and priests in vestments. Indeed, the main variation from the established norm of the Church of England was in a more formal direction, replacing Morning Prayer with weekly Holy Communion. However, the wording of the administration of Communion proved tricky to translate into Zulu, so variants were introduced.

The jewels in the crown of Anglican mission were mass baptisms and confirmations of converts. In India, the small kingdom of Travancore in southern Kerala reported 132 baptized converts in a year; not to be outdone, the Bishop of Madras confirmed 313 in one day. Worship using the *Book of Common Prayer* endowed converts with a higher order of Britishness. New churches with local leaders signalled the formal completion of imperial inculturation.

The first translation of the *Book of Common Prayer* into Urdu was published in Calcutta in 1814. The translator, Henry Martyn (1781–1812), became a missionary himself. He sought ordination and served as curate in Cambridge under Charles Simeon (1759–1836), one of the founders of the CMS. Martyn became chaplain to the East India Company and arrived in India in April 1806. A talented linguist, he translated the New Testament into Urdu, as well as producing Persian translations of the Psalms.

On occasion, the imposition of the *Book of Common Prayer* crossed over into a conscious act of Anglican imperialism in relation to other Protestant traditions. Up to the 1830s, Tamil congregations in south India came under the influence of Prussian and Danish Lutherans such as C. F. Schwartz (1726–98). Suddenly, a soft ecumenism between Halle, Copenhagen, and London gave way to an English-dominated evangelism dominated by the SPG and CMS. The German missionary C. T. E Rhenius (1790–1838) objected: 'when my fellow-labourer and I were sent out to India, now twenty-one years ago, no question was ever put to us on the subject of conformity to the Church of England'. Tamil Lutherans and Pietists were 'converted' overnight into Anglicans, indoctrinated by its *Book of Common Prayer*. They complained that their familiar Tamil scripture had been taken away from them. Indeed, other aspects of the Anglican enforcement were more persecutory: Christians were forcibly integrated into one caste and all who refused to comply were excommunicated from the Eucharist; traditional flowers were prohibited for festivals, weddings, and funerals; and Tamil lyrics and Tamil music were removed from worship.

The *Book of Common Prayer* spread with the reach of colonial ambition, so that just as the sun never set, so Evensong never ended in the British Empire. The first translation of the *Book of Common Prayer* into Chinese was the edition of Morning and Evening Prayer in 1818 by Robert Morrison (1782–1834), of the London Missionary Society. In India, versions appeared in Tamil in 1802, in Urdu in 1814, and in Bengali in 1840. There was a *Book of Common Prayer* in Maori in 1830; in Malay in 1856; in Swahili in 1876. In some cases, this would be the first appearance of a printed book in that language, so that a claim has been made for a cultural as well as religious legacy.

Sometimes translation and adaptation provoked a paradoxical sensitivity to local identities. However, always with the promise of education and evangelism came the threat of monocultural uniformity. This was true whatever the ethnicity of the colony. In early colonial Australia, the *Book of Common Prayer* had a monopoly in religion. In a church with a severe shortage of clergy, the presence of the book took the place of a minister, and services were administered by an army officer or other official. High mortality rates meant people were grateful for the rites of the Burial of the Dead, or else the Churching of Women when a mother survived childbirth. However, the book was also state sanctioned and brooked no rivals, even though many of the colonists were convicts from Catholic Ireland or Presbyterian Scotland. Roman Catholic burials were not permitted in Australia before 1820.

In that way, it is grimly appropriate that a *Book of Common Prayer* once owned by Captain James Cook (1728–79) recently went on display in an Australian museum. While not notably religious, Cook was a passive carrier of the established religion from Australia to New Zealand to Hawaii. The claim of Anglicanism to represent all Englishness was as false globally as it was at home, for the English abroad were as likely to be Catholic or Baptist as Church of England. If the *Book of Common Prayer* sounds as English as afternoon tea, like tea it conceals a more sinister economic and ethnographic history.

Chapter 6
Modernity and the
Book of Common Prayer

Modernity appears to be the natural enemy of the *Book of Common Prayer*. In 1964, after 400 years of use, a commission was established by the General Synod of the Church of England, 'to plan and prepare a revised *Book of Common Prayer*, either in stages or as a whole'. In 1967 the Church of England introduced in pamphlet form a new liturgy enigmatically called 'Series 2'. 'Series 3' followed in 1971, in which God was for the first time addressed by Anglicans as 'you'. In 1980, the *Alternative Service Book* formalized the changes in a full-scale printed book.

Many people, used to the old book, went into mourning, not only for the life of prayer which the book embodied, but for its language, which was held up as a consummate example of English prose writing. A battle to the death was drawn between traditionalists, who regarded many of the verbal experiments as banal; and innovators, for whom it was axiomatic that only modern forms of speech could be appropriate for a new age. Congregations fought a culture war over language for a generation, with intense passion on both sides, and even divided into two factions, with services for families using the new forms, while traditional rites prevailed in the early morning or in choral Evensong in cathedrals. The publication of *Common Worship* in 2000 may be called the death knell of the *Book of Common Prayer*, since it was only in that year that the old uniform order was officially replaced.

However, all is not quite as it seems. *Common Worship* also ensured the survival of Morning Prayer, Evening Prayer, and Holy Communion in their precise 1662 format, as permitted alternatives. In 2000, as opposed to 1980, there was also a linguistic revisionism back in the direction of prayer book tradition: sometimes (as in the Collects) in respect for Cranmer's original phrasing; sometimes in a cultural instinct that found grammatical formality more in keeping with ritual prayer, even as attempts were made to be more inclusive in relation to gender, race, sexuality, or urban context.

The biggest change in *Common Worship* lay not in replacing the *Book of Common Prayer* outright, as its many defenders feared, but in abolishing uniformity. The new book not only contains two different ways of celebrating Communion, but also alternative prayers within them. In other places it provides a compilation of sources taken from all over the world, with a guide to how to select and shape them. Congregations are encouraged to experiment and to improvise, in ways which would have shocked Cranmer, and horrified Laud. As a result, while the old book contains around 500 pages, the new one has over 3,500 (in a series of volumes).

Revision and change

However, it is not the case that an effort to revise the 1662 *Book of Common Prayer* was a 20th-century invention. A full-scale revision was first proposed in 1689, with the Glorious Revolution. The new Dutch King William III was mortified by English Protestantism. At his coronation he refused to kiss the Bible, as he was required. He found English forms reminiscent of Catholic ritual. There was also a political desire to bring back into the fold many of the ministers who had been excluded in 1662. Yet change proved difficult to agree on. The real question lurking here, rather than whether it was right to replace the book in the 1960s, is how the same text survived for 300 years before that, word for word, and often comma for comma.

Accretion was permitted. A number of new services attached themselves to the book in the 17th century—strange Stuart polemics dressed up as penitential services to atone for the Gunpowder Plot, and the execution of Charles I; and to give thanks for the restoration of Charles II. Salvation from the Great Fire of London attracted similar thanksgiving. The Articles of Religion began to be attached to editions of the *Book of Common Prayer* proper, and *A Form of Consecrating Churches* in 1714. Alongside these 'state services' inside the book, hundreds of special acts of worship were authorized to pray in times of war or epidemic, or to give thanks for military victories or royal weddings. The Jacobite risings, the French Revolution and Napoleonic Wars, the world wars of the 20th century, all brought the English people together in 'state prayer'.

Change to the body of the *Book of Common Prayer*, on the other hand, was subject to a taboo in favour of the status quo. The axis between ceremonial and anti-ceremonial interpretations of the Anglican tradition never went away, and too much was at stake to allow even small victories on either side. Consensus lay in conservatism, with a policy of less equals more. Between 1857 and 1863, sixty-six pamphlets were published with detailed proposals. However, the only result was that in 1859 the 'state services' for the Gunpowder Plot and so on were abolished, replaced with a single service celebrating the accession of the current monarch. In 1877, a committee met to report on the punctuation of the 1662 book; it took fifteen years to make proposals, which even so were not imposed.

Attachment to the Church of England in the 18th and 19th centuries meant different things. As early as the 1690s, the term 'high church' identified a faction that was Tory in politics (opposed to the exclusion of James II), and in religion stressed continuity with Catholic tradition. Tories often emphasized ritual and priestly authority. Bishops and deans, on the other hand, were called 'latitudinarian' when they favoured a broad interpretation of practice to attract congregations. Latitudinarians tended to be Whig in politics (supporters of William III and in due course anti-Jacobite) although this was not always the case. Many clergy in local parishes were evangelical, following the success of the Methodist movement of John Wesley (1703–91). Wesley was anti-ceremonial, desiring liturgy as far as possible to imitate reading of scripture.

Fiction in the period puts ritual on a pedestal then knocks it off. Jonathan Swift (1667–1745), an Anglo-Irish clergyman in Catholic Ireland, finding himself to have only one parishioner, prays 'Dearly beloved Roger—the scripture moveth you and me in sundry places'. (James Joyce (1882–1941), as irreverent as he was anti-English, quoted this in *Finnegans Wake*.) James Boswell reports Samuel Johnson (1709–84) learning a Collect from a prayer book by heart at the age of three; nonetheless, the adult Johnson, Tory and High Church, aspired to be a guardian of morals as much as rituals. In *Tristram Shandy*, Laurence Sterne (1713–68), a latitudinarian clergyman in Anglican Yorkshire, has Mrs Shandy refer to the monthly Communion as 'Sacrament Sunday'. In *Joseph Andrews* by Henry Fielding (1707–54), the hero carries Lady Booby's prayer book to church, so the vicar questions him on religion over a glass of ale. In another direction, parodying an evangelical sermon in *Shamela*, Fielding has Parson Williams speak to the text, 'Be not Righteous over-much'.

In 1829, the Emancipation Act finally removed the public bar preventing Catholics from taking office. However, the *Book of Common Prayer* still marked a social and political division between conformism and non-conformism. For Baptists or Unitarians it was a foreign language. Yet even inside the Church of England there was disagreement. The intellectual culture in the universities stressed the closeness of the Church of England to a mainstream Catholic tradition. *Tracts for the Times*, a series of publications from 1833 to 1841, closed with an article by John Henry Newman (1801–90) arguing that the Thirty-Nine Articles were in concord with Roman Catholic doctrine. The Tractarian revival led by John Keble (1792–1866) stressed the centrality of the *Book of Common Prayer*, but interpreted in a ceremonial style: eastward-facing celebration of Communion, candles and cross at the altar, Eucharistic vestments, and incense.

The Gothic revival in architecture assisted, by following a medieval ritual design, with chancel removed from the nave and the altar raised on steps, often with space for choir stalls. Old churches were refurbished in this pattern as well as new ones. Many British churches today have apparently medieval features invented by Victorians.

Keble's *The Christian Year* was the most widely known book of English poems in the 19th century. Its preface promised an emotional index for what he called 'the sober standard of feeling' expressed in the official liturgy. Yet the Church of England was also home to the ministry of Charles Kingsley (1819–75), Christian socialist and historical novelist. He vigorously opposed the high church politics of E. B. Pusey (1800–82), professor of Hebrew, leader of the Oxfordians, and promoter of Eucharistic religion combined with a revival of auricular confession. Kingsley's vision of Anglicanism by contrast was of a manly and socially committed Christianity, comprehensive and democratic.

Over such conflicts lay the shroud of the crisis in faith by which the authority of scripture was doubted in relation to the tenets of new sciences. In *Middlemarch* by George Eliot (1819–80), Lydgate is told 'But now, if you speak out of the Prayer-book itself, you are liable to be contradicted'. Yet questioning the existence of God is not incompatible here with a Christian moral discipline that harked back to the evangelicalism of Eliot's low church Anglican family.

Newman's conversion to Roman Catholicism in 1845 confirmed for many outside the Oxford Movement its anti-Protestant bias, and a backlash ensued. Evangelicals sneered at their opponents as 'ritualists', encouraging bishops to enforce the letter of the prayer book rubrics against them. In Birmingham, for example, Father Richard Enraght (1837–98) advocated the wearing of chasuble and alb, the use of candles at the altar and of Communion wafers, and bowing the head during the *Gloria*, all of which his bishop forbade. In 1880, he was prosecuted and put in prison. However, this punishment was considered outrageously disproportionate, and turned public opinion the other way.

Controversy continued until the outbreak of World War I. In Germany, copies of Goethe's *Faust* and even Friedrich Nietzsche's *Thus Spoke Zarathustra* (with its famous phrase, 'God is dead!') vied with the New Testament as books for the Western Front. English Tommies often took to Flanders a *Book of Common Prayer* (perhaps in the shortened form of the *Soldier's Prayer Book*). Copies survive strewn with bullets or shrapnel, or with poignant inscriptions ('a small present from the Somme'). As the bodies of young soldiers piled up, a different wave of emotion surrounded the prayer book. Bishops received letters from agonized families who desired to pray for their dead, but were refused by ministers sticking to the letter of the Order for the Burial of the Dead. Increasingly the language of the 16th century was felt not to match contemporary needs. Military chaplains reported that working class soldiers felt alienated by a form of words that they did not understand.

When Parliament finally met in 1927 to discuss the proposed *Revised Prayer Book*, however, they found a jumble of measures designed to please different sides. The interests of the working class were not high on this list. Ritualists, including the liturgical scholar, W. H. Frere (1863–1938), Bishop of Truro and author of a distinguished *History of the Book of Common Prayer*, managed to negotiate some returns to the 1549 and 1637 (Scottish) versions of Communion, such as an *epiclesis* (calling of the Holy Spirit into the elements of bread and wine). There were prayers for the departed; at the same time the number of prayers for the king was reduced.

Evangelical opponents wrote to their Members of Parliament
to voice their objections. The Home Secretary, Arthur Henderson
(1863–1935), was himself an evangelical. Parliament in any case
contained many non-conformists, for instance in Wales or Scotland,
who were shocked to find a version of Holy Communion so close
(in their eyes) to transubstantiation. God forbid a United Kingdom
that was not explicitly Protestant. A classic collision between
church and state ensued: the bishops agreed the new book, but
Parliament voted it down. Undeterred, in 1958 bishops allowed
its use in parishes. Royal weddings, up to the Prince of Wales
with Lady Diana Spencer, and the Duke of Cambridge with Kate
Middleton, used a 1928 text, even as TV mistakenly called it 1662.

The language of the *Book of Common Prayer*

Again and again in the history of the *Book of Common Prayer*,
public arguments about its contents have been conducted by
members of the clergy, and have concentrated, it might be thought
to the point of obsession, on the meaning of the Eucharist. One of
the features of 20th-century movements in relation to the liturgy,
by contrast, has been a voice for laity. Yet here there is also
paradox, for the laity, when asked, often spoke in favour of the
Book of Common Prayer. This came from unexpected quarters.
In 1957, Archbishop Geoffrey Fisher (1887–1972) called to order
a committee at Lambeth Palace to revise the Psalter, including
eminent lay experts on literary language like C. S. Lewis
(1898–1963) and T. S. Eliot (1888–1965). Lewis, a medievalist
and self-professed enemy of modernism, turned out nonetheless
to be more in favour of linguistic change than Eliot, the apostle
of modernist poetry. What did you do today, Valerie Eliot asked
her husband on return from one of the committee's meetings.
'I think I may have saved the Twenty-Third Psalm.'

Eliot by the 1960s was a pillar of the establishment and a
longstanding churchwarden at St Stephen's Church, Gloucester
Road in London. He described himself as an 'Anglo-Catholic'.

His defence of traditional language is part of a high church profile, except that it pervades his poetic modernism quite as thoroughly as his public positions:

> Because I do not hope to turn again
> Because I do not hope
> Because I do not hope to turn

This is the opening of *Ash Wednesday*, a long poem written shortly after his conversion in 1927. It appears to be spoken from the point of view of a person who lacked faith in the past but strives to move towards God. The first line translates a love poem by the 13th-century Italian poet Guido Cavalcanti. Later lines imitate Dante's *Purgatorio* and Shakespeare's *Sonnet* 29. The poem is also suffused by what is transparently a language taken from traditional prayer: 'Pray for us now and at the hour of our death'; 'Speak the word only'; 'Suffer me not to be separated'; 'And let my cry come unto thee'. The first of these phrases is from the *Ave Maria*; the second from the gospel of Matthew in the King James Version; the third is from an ancient prayer, the *Anima Christi*; and the last (slightly adapted) from the Litany in the *Book of Common Prayer*.

It might be thought, then, that the poem is a kind of modern prayer. Yet at no point does the poem pretend to be the expression of a particular form of faith. If anything, the subject of the poem inhabits a space as far off from its object at the end as at the beginning. The poem is a state of feeling, not a statement of doctrine. Its use of traditional language of prayer has the same timbre or pitch, of apprehension not achievement. Prayer expresses despair or lack of grace as readily as it does faith.

In 1968, W. H. Auden (1907–73) also agreed to sit on a committee devoted to making liturgy more accessible to modern congregations. While Eliot made the journey from New England to London to do so, Auden's pilgrimage was in the opposite direction, the request coming from the Episcopal Church in New York. His hosts were unnerved when he replied that he would do so on condition that the 16th-century language of Cranmer and Coverdale be left unchanged. A demand for liturgical change came not from the laity, he said, but from priests hoping to attract the young by looking trendy. Grumpy old man aside, he expressed a more serious argument in a letter in 1971: 'The Rite—preaching, of course, is another matter—is the link between the dead and the unborn. This calls for a timeless language which, in practice, means a dead language.' Contemporaneity, Auden suggests, is not the criterion for an authentic language of prayer. It consists instead in a language which is felt to be shared across the ages.

In one sense Auden appeals here to a model of liturgy in which it is precisely its function to speak across or even outside of time. Liturgical language is peculiar in that it is poised in a continuously present tense. What is said now can be said and will be said in the same way at any other time, and has been for centuries. All liturgical writers have borrowed from past versions in the hope that they carry within themselves the presence of the past. The *Book of Common Prayer* did both more, and less, than translate Sarum. The Reformers destroyed the medieval rite, and yet transposed it freely for their own uses. Their Victorian Anglo-Catholic successors argued in reverse that 1549 was the Roman rite *redivivus*. Catholic tradition trusts to an unbroken line of transmission, although the story is more complex than that. Modern study of the rituals of the Greek and Coptic and other early churches has broken down the notion of a unified 'Christian liturgy'. Yet ritual in and between these many languages is a cognitive palimpsest. Morning Prayer and Baptism in the *Book of Common Prayer* contain words reaching back to the first years of the Roman Empire, and in some cases hundreds of years earlier, to the rituals of Jewish communities three thousand years ago.

Auden believed, however, that the *Book of Common Prayer* was not only timeless but timely. It 'was compiled at the ideal historical moment, that is to say, when the English Language was already in all essentials the language we use now'. It never sounded like a dead language, even centuries later, in Auden's own time; in the same way that actors make Shakespeare comprehensible in a present day theatre. And yet it was a language that still 'possessed what our own has almost totally lost, a sense for the ceremonial and ritual'. Like Eliot, Auden found it natural to borrow liturgical idiom in poems for his time:

> Holy this moment, wholly in the right,
> As, in complete obedience
> To the light's laconic outcry, next
> As a sheet, near as a wall,
> Out there as a mountain's poise of stone,
> The world is present, about,
> And I know that I am, here, not alone

This is from 'Prime', written in August 1949, later published in *Horae Canonicae*. The title mimics the divine office of the Breviary (see Chapter 1). The canonical hours, Auden felt, gave to everyday life a universal structure. Far from being an incidental feature of a long-lost monastic discipline, they are a profound grounding metaphor in human experience. This was just one of the ways in which prayer meant for him something beyond a confessional framework. In an essay, 'Work, Carnival and Prayer', Auden wrote: 'To pray is to pay attention or, shall we say, to "listen" to someone or something other than oneself.' Prayer is not a specialized religious language, but a human form.

The shock of the old

Mortality was much on Auden's mind in 1971. The 'link between the dead and the unborn' was a frequent experience as he attended funerals of friends from his youth or middle age, and foresaw his own decline (he died in 1973). In this he regularly encountered the words of the burial service in the *Book of Common Prayer* (Box 11).

Box 11 From the Order for the Burial of the Dead, 1662

When they come to the grave, while the corps is made ready to be laid into the earth, the Priest shall say, or the Priest and Clerks shall sing,

Man that is born of a woman, hath but a short time to live, and is full of misery. He cometh up, and is cut down like a flower; he fleeth as it were a shadow, and never continueth in one stay.

In the midst of life we are in death: of whom may we seek for succour, but of thee, O Lord, who for our sins art justly displeased?

Yet, O Lord God most holy, O Lord most mighty, O holy and most merciful Saviour, deliver us not into the bitter pains of eternal death.

Thou knowest, Lord, the secrets of our hearts; shut not thy merciful ears to our prayer; but spare us, Lord most holy, O God most mighty, O holy and merciful Saviour, thou most worthy Judge eternal, suffer us not at our last hour for any pains of death to fall from thee.

Then while the earth shall be cast upon the body by some standing by, the Priest shall say,

Forasmuch as it hath pleased Almighty God of his great mercy to take unto himself the soul of our dear *brother* here departed, we therefore commit *his* body to the ground; earth to earth, ashes to ashes, dust to dust, in sure and certain hope of the resurrection to eternal life, through our Lord Jesus Christ, who shall change our vile body, that it may be like unto his glorious body, according to the mighty working, whereby he is able to subdue all things to himself. (OWC, 455)

This text in 1662 survives verbatim from 1549. It is neither free composition nor exact quotation. It begins with a series of scriptural citations rendering into English a textual (and often musical) sequence found in the Sarum *Manuale*. This does not appear anywhere in the Roman rite and can be thought of as distinctively English. The section 'In the midst of life we are in death', on the other hand, is taken from an anthem by the 9th-century German poet Notker. It was a popular dirge all over Germany through the Middle Ages, and Luther wrote a hymn on the basis of it, 'Mitten wir im Leben sind', widespread after the Reformation. It was translated into English by Coverdale, whose *Ghostly Psalms* provides the immediate source for Cranmer. The custom of casting earth on a coffin goes back long before Christianity, for instance in Horace's *Odes* (1.28.35). The exquisite English phrase, 'Earth to earth, ashes to ashes, dust to dust' translates directly Sarum Latin: *terram terrae: cinerem cineri: pulverum pulveri*. Even here Cranmer recalled old English stock: 'Erthe unto erthe' is a phrase in a medieval lyric.

This is therefore a good example of what Auden means by a language that is neither new nor old, or else forever new, by being so old. The opening section of the most famous English poem of the 20th century, Eliot's *The Waste Land* (1922), is called 'The Burial of the Dead'. These fragments are shored against our ruins. The language of the new versions of the 1960s sometimes struggled for such a natural idiom. An example is the Lord's Prayer: 'Hallowed be your name'. The pronoun is insistently changed, whereas the fussy residual subjunctive form 'be' is retained, along with a past participle that has been in disuse in everyday conversation for centuries. The same happens to the response used in Morning Prayer (and elsewhere) to the acclamation, 'The Lord be with you'. In 1549 this is given as 'And with thy spirite'. For some reason in 1971 it was thought appropriate to reply instead, 'And also with you', a phrase nobody has ever used anywhere else. Imagine saying that at breakfast, when asked for the milk.

Nevertheless, the little word 'you' is a watershed in the history of the *Book of Common Prayer*. Before 1960 it was unthinkable to change the curious vestigial form 'thou', when addressing God in formal Anglican prayer. Since then it has become unthinkable not to. From this change everything else follows. Probably no change has been so commonly and powerfully misunderstood. The use of the pronoun 'thou/thy' in relation to God became for traditional Anglicans the most distinctive and precious feature of the archaism of prayer book English. They prized it because it sounded reassuringly old-fashioned, and also because it seemed to have the proper element of respect and formality in addressing God. Yet this is precisely the opposite of its meaning in the 16th century. In the case of God, using 'thou' was established by long precedent in Middle English devotional material, as in the Lord's Prayer. As a general rule, as with the modern French *tu*, 'thou' in Middle English signified familiarity or intimacy, as opposed to the more formal 'you' or *vous*. It was a word you used to your children or to your partner in bed. As a word to God it signified closeness and ardency. However, it was also slightly risky, since the general rule is subject to social valencies. By the same token, in the right context, 'thou' could be used transgressively or as a sign of disrespect, for instance by a servant to a master. As any reader of Shakespeare knows, the 16th century was prone to pronoun-switching, by which one register could be exchanged for another. Using 'thou' could be a verbal habit of a more powerful person to a lesser one, to convey ease; it could be used in sudden flirting affection; it could be a threat. Every French teenager knows how to play the game of *tutoyer*, saying *tu* when *vous* is correct.

Alas, the social miracle of the second-person pronoun is lost to modern English. However, the revisers were right in thinking that there is no longer any point in echoing a parody of the old subtlety, especially since 'thou' was now being used to reinforce English snobbishness and nostalgia, when they hardly needed any encouragement. Changing to 'you' was inevitable and common sense. In its wake, though, it brought further and more testing linguistic concerns. Many of these experiments were first tried out far away from the United Kingdom. The church in New Zealand abandoned the use of 'thou', 'thee', and 'thine' in 1966. It encouraged a wider range of language in relation to God, who is once even called 'father and mother of us all'. Inclusive language was favoured, and no masculine pronouns are used for God in the Psalms.

Careful thought was given to language in revising the American *Book of Common Prayer* in 1979. Modernization fretted against the fear that worshippers might not like the updated language. Therefore, two versions were produced for the Burial Service, Daily Office, and Eucharist, one in contemporary language and another in more traditional style. However, rites such as Ordination, Baptism, and Marriage were drawn up in modern language to ensure that participants understood what they were undertaking.

There was some attempt at inclusive language. For example, in the Nicene Creed 'for us men and for our salvation' became 'for us and for our salvation'. Moreover, biblical references were rendered more accurately, often leading to more inclusive language. In the *Gloria*, for instance, 'on earth peace, good will towards men' became 'and peace to his people on earth'. Elsewhere, masculine pronouns were italicized so that they could be replaced with feminine pronouns, notably in the service for consecration of bishops, a decade before the first woman was consecrated in the Episcopal Church of the USA.

In many cases, progressive change in the wording of the liturgy preceded political change in the Anglican worldwide Communion. In this it made some attempt to atone for language which for centuries had been misogynist, racist, and homophobic. Just one example in the original *Book of Common Prayer* was the service for the churching of women. This was originally a rite of bodily purification for the child-bearing woman to re-enter sacred ground, something even 17th-century English clergymen became embarrassed by, and so turned into a service of thanksgiving. Other innovations occurred first in Africa and Asia. The earliest stirrings of Eucharistic revivalism—recentring worship around this one weekly sacrament—came in Zanzibar and Northern Rhodesia (later Zambia). The Church of South India sought community involvement in Communion as early as 1950, making intercession extempore, and allowing lay people to initiate prayer. Mid-morning Communion broke the hegemony of Morning Prayer.

The beginning of the end

While traditionalists lampooned new liturgies for verbal infelicity (often with good reason) more profound change loomed in relation to the original structural principles of the *Book of Common Prayer*: uniformity, rigidity, and hierarchy. The *Book of Common Prayer* is a Tudor creation, and the Tudors loved such things. Whether in the Elizabethan church, or in the Civil Wars, in the colonization of Ireland, or the extension of the British Empire to the ends of the earth, the *Book of Common Prayer* always operated as an instrument of monolithic social order, whatever its aspiration to spiritual enlightenment. This alone made it difficult for it to survive into the 21st century. The strain is evident as the end approaches. A generation after Auden, Geoffrey Hill (1932–2016), in his long poem *Speech! Speech!* (2000), refers warily to:

INORDINATE wording of Common Prayer

The pun on 'ordination' fights with a sense that language is no longer equal to the task. It is as if the centre cannot hold. As the millennium ended, Rowan Williams (b.1950) commented on the concealed polemic of the *Book of Common Prayer*, a capacity to 'say or not say certain things'. His consecration as Archbishop of

Canterbury in 2002 was the first since Cardinal Reginald Pole (1500–58) where this book did not hold sole authority.

The most interesting modern enemy of the *Book of Common Prayer* was Gregory Dix (1901–52). He was that eccentric Church of England re-invention, an Anglican Benedictine, as well as a notable Anglo-Catholic priest. In 1945, he published a work of classical importance on ritual, *The Shape of the Liturgy*. Its ambitions lay beyond the Church of England, synthesizing all Christian liturgy in order to understand its fundamental structure.

It is a beautifully written book, never afraid to be provocative. At a stroke it scotched a number of Anglican pious myths. Far from Anglo-Catholic, he saw the 1549 text as Zwinglian. Subsequent scholarship has vindicated him in showing Cranmer adopted Swiss views on the Eucharist by 1547, if more Bullinger than Zwingli. However, Dix did not share either in a search for a more ancient model of Eucharistic purity. He did not believe in the existence of an as yet undiscovered primitive form of prayer, because he did not believe that *text* was fundamental to liturgy. Liturgy, he said, is more a matter of doing than it is of saying. Reflecting on the scriptural command of Jesus, 'do this in remembrance of me', Dix remarked:

> Was ever another command so obeyed? For century after century…this action has been done, in every conceivable human circumstance, for every conceivable human need from infancy and before it to extreme old age and after it.

Dix called Cranmer's version of Communion 'a vivid mental remembering of the passion'. The error was fundamental, he felt: for it is not necessary to believe in transubstantiation to see the Eucharist as more than re-evocation of the past. *Something is done*, something good enough for a king at a crowning, or a criminal at the scaffold. Like any action, it is determined by process, what Dix calls its 'shape', here fourfold: taking, blessing, breaking, and giving. Dix argued that the 1662 rite ruptured this social contract. It does not need reforming in order to bring it up to date, but to make it whole again. For this to be fulfilled, Dix required what he called a 'people's liturgy': an explicitly embodied relationship between priest and laity. Although he died of cancer aged fifty, he shaped all the Anglican liturgical revolutions that followed. However, they were interpreted differently: while the church in south India hoped thereby to find union with the free churches, Dix himself sought reunion with Rome.

In the 1960s, Archbishop Michael Ramsey (1904–88) presided over a Church of England uncomfortable with its status as the established national religion, and ready to experiment with liturgy. It is striking in this respect that the passing of the *Book of Common Prayer* coincided almost exactly with that of its nemesis, the Tridentine Mass, prescribed after the Council of Trent by Pope Pius V in 1570.

The two books have more in common than might be thought. Both are products of authoritarianism in the face of profound social and political change. Each attempted to unify traditions that had previously proliferated in local variation. Both succeeded in creating a form of words and rubrics that not only lasted, but subverted the attempts of future revisers. Supporters of each book have also shared a venom for the perpetration of their demise, lasting well over a generation, in which change itself is execrated as a sign of liberalization and secularization.

As with the *Book of Common Prayer*, the most divisive aspect of the new Roman Catholic liturgies was language—the end to 2,000 years of continuous worship in Latin, 1,500 years after the end of the Roman Empire, and a thousand after it ceased to be a common spoken language. However, for the Second Vatican Council of 1962, the key point was not modernizing for its own sake, but rediscovering the laity as the true body of Christ.

It is a powerful irony of history that the Latin rite of Roman Catholicism came to an end in the same decade as the vernacular rite that defeated it in the English-speaking world. If that expresses a narrowly anglocentric world view, it should be recalled that the British Empire magnified the effect of the *Book of Common Prayer* beyond anything imagined in Westminster Hall in December 1548.

From the beginnings of printing to the dawn of the digital age (with short interruptions under Mary I and Oliver Cromwell) this book has lasted nearly 500 years. There were over 500 editions of the *Book of Common Prayer* between 1549 and the 1730s; an estimated average print run of 2,500 to 3,000 suggests well over a million copies in circulation in this period. With new technology these numbers increased exponentially. At its height, in the decade from 1836 to 1846, the three official printers produced nearly half a million copies between them per year. The *Book of Common Prayer* has been used from Canada to Brazil, from the West Indies to Nigeria, from Kenya to Bangladesh, from Sri Lanka to New Zealand. Translations appeared in Hindi, Urdu, and Tamil; Maasai and Hausa; Cantonese, Japanese, Burmese, and Vietnamese; Arabic and Persian; and Fijian, Maori, and three types of Inuit.

Praise of the book, whether of the glories of its language, or its place in human community, is easy to exaggerate. Depending on your point of view, its success has come down to being in the right (or wrong) place in history. Yet its translatability also has something to do with the strength and flexibility of its rhythm and diction, as also its care of gesture in demarcating the boundaries of human feeling.

Cranmer may not be a celebrated writer, but he knew how to read, how to compile, and how to edit. 'Lighten our darkness, we beseech thee, O Lord'; 'Almighty God, unto whom all hearts are open, all desires known, and from whom no secrets are hid';

'Earth to earth, ashes to ashes, dust to dust'. Cranmer had as exact a sense of the English language as anyone. When David Bowie (1947–2016) looked back on the 1970s, and summed up its revolutions in music, culture, sex, drugs, and identity, he sang the chorus, 'Ashes to ashes, funk to funky', without feeling that any of these words was out of place, in space or in time.

References

Chapter 1: Ritual and the Reformation

The Rites of Durham is quoted from the edition by J. T. Fowler, Surtees Society, 107 (Durham, 1902), p. 8; the authorship is questioned in the forthcoming edition by Margaret Harvey. Accounts of medieval English liturgy are taken from Eamon Duffy, *Stripping of the Altars*, 2nd edition (New Haven, 2005), quotations pp. 91 and 97; Richard W. Pfaff, *The Liturgy in Medieval England: A History* (Cambridge, 2009), quotation pp. 7–8; and Miri Rubin, *Corpus Christi: The Eucharist in Late Medieval Culture* (Cambridge, 1991); quotations, pp. 58 and 26. I have used the editions of the Sarum Missal by Wickham Legg and the York Missal by W. G. Henderson. Quotations from *The Boke of Margery Kempe* are from Barry Windeatt's edition (Harlow, 2000), p. 321; *The Paston Letters*, ed. Norman Davis (Oxford, 1999), p. 36; John Mirk, *Festial*, ed. Powell, 1: 154. The argument about changes in 16th-century ritual is indebted to John Bossy, *Christianity in the West, 1400–1700* (Oxford, 1985); quotations from pp. 67, 66, 27. On the Books of Hours see Duffy, *Marking the Hours: English People and their Prayers* (New Haven, 2006). Use has been made of the accounts of the continental Reformation in Euan Cameron, *The European Reformation*, 2nd edition (Oxford, 2012); of the English Reformation in Duffy, *Stripping of the Altars*; and Ethan Shagan, *Popular Politics and the English Reformation* (Cambridge, 2003). Information on Reformed liturgies in Germany and Switzerland is taken from Nathan Mitchell's chapter in *The Oxford History of Christian Worship*, ed. G. Wainwright (Oxford, 2006). I am grateful to the libraries of Cambridge University,

Trinity College, Cambridge, Lambeth Palace, and York Minster, for permission to consult the manuscript and early printed copies referred to.

Chapter 2: The making of the *Book of Common Prayer*

Quotations from Luther are from the Philadelphia Edition of *Luther's Works*; from Erasmus, from the Toronto *Collected Works*. References to early English sources are taken from *The Godly Order: Texts and Studies Relating to the Book of Common Prayer*, ed. Geoffrey Cuming, Alcuin Club (London, 1983); and Charles Butterworth, *The English Primers (1529–1545)* (Philadelphia, 1953). Cranmer's part in negotiation and composition for the 1549 and 1552 books is recounted from Diarmaid MacCulloch, *Thomas Cranmer: A Life* (New Haven, 1996); and in MacCulloch, *Reformation: Europe's House Divided 1490–1700* (London, 2004). Accounts of the Prebendaries' Plot are given from opposite points of view in Duffy, *Stripping of the Altars*; and Shagan, *Popular Politics*. The account of Protestant feeling here is much influenced by Margaret Aston, especially *England's Iconoclasts* (Oxford, 1988) and *Broken Idols* (Cambridge, 2016). The printing history of the Prayer Book is being transformed by Peter Blayney's history of *The Stationers' Company and the Printers of London 1501–1557* (Cambridge, 2013). The Prayer Book Rebellion is covered in Anthony Fletcher and Diarmaid MacCulloch, *Tudor Rebellions*, 5th edition (London, 2004); the quotation from Hooker's *Description of the City of Exeter* is on p. 54. Bucer's comment on the 1549 edition is from *Martin Bucer and the Book of Common Prayer*, ed. E. C. Whitaker, Alcuin Club (Great Wakering, 1974). Official Tudor documents are from *Tudor Royal Proclamations*, ed. P. Hughes and J. Larkin, 3 vols (New Haven, 1964–9), and David Wilkins, *Concilia Magnae Britanniae*, 4 vols (London, 1737); quotations from 3: 861–3. Interventions of bishops are cited from *Visitation Articles and Injunctions of the Period of the Reformation*, ed. W. H. Frere and W. M. Kennedy, 3 vols (London, 1910).

Chapter 3: Word, body, and gesture

On Dürer's 'Praying Hands', see Norbert Wolf, *Albrecht Dürer 1471–1528: Das Genie der deutschen Renaissance* (Cologne, 2006). Wittgenstein calls man *ein zeremonielles Tier* in 'Bemerkungen über Frazers *Golden Bough*/Remarks on Frazer's *Golden Bough*', in

Philosophical Occasions, 1912–1951, ed. James Klagge and Alfred Nordmann (Indianapolis, 1993), p. 129. See also Wendy James's introduction to the anthropology of ritual, *The Ceremonial Animal* (Oxford, 2003). I am indebted to the general discussion of Protestant culture in Euan Cameron, *Enchanted Europe: Superstition, Reason, and Religion, 1250–1750* (Oxford, 2010), esp. pp. 58–62; Patrick Collinson, *The Birthpangs of Protestant England* (London, 1988) and *The Religion of Protestants* (Oxford, 1982); and Alexandra Walsham, especially *The Reformation of the Landscape* (Oxford, 2012). Citations from Bucer are from *Enarrationes in evangelia* (Straßburg, 1527); from Calvin, *Institutes*, 2 vols, ed. J. McNeill and F. Battles (Philadelphia, 1960), ii.854; from Thomas More, *Answer to the First Part of a Poisoned Book* (London, 1533), sig. 6r. Reference to Chaderton is indebted to Peter Lake, *Moderate Puritans and the Elizabethan Church* (Cambridge, 1982). The quotations from Roy A. Rappaport, *Ritual and Religion in the Making of Humanity* (Cambridge, 1999), are from pp. 31 and 40; that from Mary Douglas, *Natural Symbols: Explorations in Cosmology*, 2nd edition (London, 1996), is from p. 2. The reference to Duffy is from *Stripping of the Altars*, p. 93. The citation from J. L. Austin comes from *How to Do Things with Words* (Oxford, 1962), pp. 5–6; *Tess of the d'Urbervilles* is cited from Simon Gatrell's Oxford World's Classics edition (2008), ch. 14; *Jane Eyre* from Margaret Smith's Oxford World's Classics edition (2000), p. 289; *Oliver Twist* from Kathleen Tillotson's Oxford World's Classics edition (2008), p. 33.

Chapter 4: Politics and religion

The reference to earlier Reformation scholarship is to A. G. Dickens, *The English Reformation*, revised edition (London, 1967); the quotation from Nicholas Tyacke, *Anti-Calvinists: The Rise of English Arminianism, 1590–1640* (Oxford, 1987) is on p. 116. The developing history of the arguments concerning the prayer book is indebted to G. J. Cuming, *A History of Anglican Liturgy* (London, 1969), from which p. 157 is quoted. On the Elizabethan and Jacobean periods, recourse has been made to Judith Maltby, *Prayer Book and People in Elizabethan and Early Stuart England* (Cambridge, 1998); on the Stuart period, to Anthony Milton, *Catholic and Reformed* (Cambridge, 2002); on the Civil War, to Michael Braddick, *God's Fury, England's Fire* (London, 2008). The citations concerning Laud are from Kenneth Fincham and Nicholas Tyacke, *Altars Restored: The Changing*

Face of English Religious Worship, 1547–c.1700 (Oxford, 2007), pp. 148
and 252; concerning events in 1660, Ronald Hutton, *The Restoration*
(Oxford, 1993), pp. 7 and 143. John Evelyn is cited from his *Diary*,
ed. E. S. de Beer, 6 vols (Oxford, 1955), iii. 203–4. Official sources
are taken from Wilkins, *Concilia*, iv. 37; *Acts of the Privy Council*, II
(1547–50), p. 291 (16 June 1549); *Journals of the House of Lords*, XI,
pp. 7–8 (reprinted in *English Historical Documents*, vi.57–8); and
XI, pp. 179–82 (*English Historical Documents*, vi.365–70). Other sources
related to liturgical history come from *Constitutions and Canons*, ed.
Wilson; and the collections by Cardwell, *History of Conferences*,
pp. 277 and 303; Cuming, *The Durham Book*, pp. 287–8; and
Cuming, *Godly Order*, p. 146 (see 'Further Reading'). Discussion of
Richard Baxter is indebted to the work of William Lamont;
quotations from Baxter are from *Reliquiae Baxterianae* (London,
1696), pp. 234 and 232.

Chapter 5: Empire and prayer book

The quotations from *Robinson Crusoe* are from the edition by
J. Richetti (London, 2001), p. 51. The prayer for the Lord Governor
of Ireland is from *The Booke of the Common Praier* (Dublin: Humfrey
Powell), sig. S4ᵛ. The discussion of Ireland includes a quotation from
Colm Lennon, *Sixteenth Century Ireland*, pp. 167–9; the concept of
'anglicization' is borrowed from Patricia Palmer, *Language and
Conquest in Early Modern Ireland* (Cambridge, 2001). On Italy, see
Stefano Villani, 'Italian Translations of the Book of Common Prayer',
in *Travels and Translations*, ed. Alison Yarrington, Stefano Villani,
and Julia Kelly (Amsterdam, 2013), pp. 303–19. In the case of North
America: references to Virginia are taken from James B. Bell, *Empire,
Religion and Revolution in Early Virginia, 1607–1786* (London,
2013); to New England from the chapter by Virginia DeJohn
Anderson, to the Carolinas to the chapter by Robert Weir, both in
Nicholas Canny, ed., *The Oxford History of the British Empire*, vol. 1,
*The Origins of Empire: British Overseas Enterprise to the Close of the
Seventeenth Century* (Oxford, 1998). First dates of translations are
from Griffiths, *Bibliography of the Book of Common Prayer* (London,
2002). Citation from the American *Book of Common Prayer* is from
M. H. Shepherd's *Oxford American Prayer Book Commentary* (New
York, 1950). The discussion of North American languages is indebted
to Adrian S. Edwards, 'Early Northern Iroquoian Language Books in
the British Library', *eBLJ* (2008), 1–24; of religion in the British

Empire to Hilary Carey, *God's Empire: Religion and Colonialism in the British World 1801–1908* (Cambridge, 2012). References to southern Africa are from Cynthia Botha's chapter in *The Oxford Guide to the Book of Common Prayer: A Worldwide Survey*, ed. Charles Hefling and Cynthia Shattuck (Oxford, 2006). Indian experience of Anglicanism is cited from Robert Eric Fykenberg, 'Christian Missions and the Raj', in Norman Etherington, ed., *Missions and Empire*, Oxford History of the British Empire Companion Series (Oxford, 2005); Australian from Michael Gladwin's essay, 'The *Book of Common Prayer* in Australia, 1788–1918', in *St Mark's Review*, 222 (2012), 75–88.

Chapter 6: Modernity and the *Book of Common Prayer*

The battle to replace the *Book of Common Prayer* is described by Colin Buchanan, 'The Winds of Change', in *The Book of Common Prayer: A Worldwide Survey*, ed. Hefling and Shattuck; I also benefited from the sections in the same book on Africa and Asia. The anecdote about Swift is reported by the Earl of Orrery in *Remarks on the Life and Writing of Dr Swift* (1751); Boswell's *Life of Johnson* is cited from the edition by G. B. Hill and L. F. Powell, 6 vols (Oxford, 2014), 1: 40; *Tristram Shandy* is cited from the Oxford World's Classics edition by Ian Campbell Ross (2009), p. 497; *Joseph Andrews* and *Shamela* are cited from the Oxford World's Classics edition by Tom Keymer (1999), pp. 18 and 324; *Middlemarch* from Rosemary Ashton's Penguin edition (1994), p. 170. Peter B. Nockles, *The Oxford Movement in Context* (Cambridge, 2008) considers the churchmanship of Newman, Keble, and Pusey; Norman Vance, *Sinews of the Spirit* (Cambridge, 1985), the alternative Victorianism of 'muscular Christianity'. The letters of C. S. Lewis and T. S. Eliot on revising the Psalter are preserved in Lambeth Palace Library. Poems by T. S. Eliot (also in Chapter 3) are quoted from *The Complete Poems and Plays* (London, 1968); by W. H. Auden from *Collected Poems* (London, 1975). Letters by Auden to Canon Charles Guilbert, 19 March 1968, and to J. Chester Johnson, 6 July 1971, are cited from Edward Mendelson, *Later Auden* (New York, 2000). The essay 'Work, Carnival and Prayer' can be found in the Appendix to *The Complete Works of W. H. Auden*, vol. 6, ed. Edward Mendelson (Princeton, 2015). The comment on Eliot's poetry is from 'Ash Wednesday', by E. E. Duncan-Jones, in B. Rajan, *T. S. Eliot: A Study of His Writings by Several Hands* (1947). Quotations from liturgical revisions are from *The Liturgy or Eucharist of the Church of the Province of New Zealand: An Alternative Order*

Approved for Experimental Use Upon Certain Conditions by the General Synod (Association of Anglican Bookrooms in New Zealand, 1966); and *The Book of Common Prayer: According to the Use of the Episcopal Church* (New York, 1979). Geoffrey Hill's poem is cited from *Broken Hierarchies* (Oxford, 2013), p. 314; Rowan Williams from *On Christian Theology* (Oxford, 2000), p. 211; Gregory Dix from *The Shape of the Liturgy* (London, 1945), p. 743. David Bowie's 'Ashes to Ashes' is quoted from my own copy of *Scary Monsters (and Super Creeps)* (1980).

The Book of Common Prayer

Further reading

Aston, Margaret, *Broken Idols of the English Reformation* (Cambridge: Cambridge University Press, 2016).

Bell, James B., *Empire, Religion and Revolution in Early Virginia, 1607–1786* (London: Palgrave, 2013).

Bond, Francis, *An Introduction to English Church Architecture*, 2 vols (Oxford: Oxford University Press, 1913).

Bossy, John, *Christianity in the West, 1400–1700* (Oxford: Oxford University Press, 1985).

Braddick, Michael, *God's Fury, England's Fire: A New History of the English Civil Wars* (London: Penguin Books, 2008).

Breviarium ad usum Sarum, ed. F. Procter and C. Wordsworth, 2 vols (Cambridge: Cambridge University Press, 1879–82) (text based on the 1531 printed edition of Sarum).

Brightman, F. E., *The English Rite*, 2 vols (London: Rivingtons, 1915).

Cameron, Euan, *The European Reformation* (Oxford: Clarendon Press, 1991).

Cameron, Euan, *Enchanted Europe: Superstition, Reason, and Religion, 1250–1750* (Oxford: Oxford University Press, 2010).

Canny, Nicholas, ed., *The Oxford History of the British Empire*, vol. 1, *The Origins of Empire: British Overseas Enterprise to the Close of the Seventeenth Century* (Oxford, 1998).

Cardwell, Edward, *A History of Conferences Connected with the Revision of the Book of Common Prayer 1558–1690* (Oxford: Oxford University Press, 1861).

Carey, Hilary, *God's Empire: Religion and Colonialism in the British World 1801–1908* (Cambridge, 2012).

Church, R. W., *The Oxford Movement: Twelve Years 1833–1845* (London: Macmillan, 1892).

Clark, Francis, S. J., *Eucharistic Sacrifice and the Reformation* (London: Darton, Longman & Todd, 1960).

Collinson, Patrick, *The Religion of Protestants: The Church in English Society 1559–1625* (Oxford: Clarendon Press, 1982).

Collinson, Patrick, *The Birthpangs of Protestant England* (London: Macmillan, 1988).

Constitutions and Canons Ecclesiastical 1604, ed. H. A. Wilson (Oxford: Clarendon Press, 1923).

Cressy, David, *Birth, Marriage and Death: Ritual, Religion and the Life-Cycle in Tudor and Stuart England* (Oxford: Oxford University Press, 1997).

Cressy, David, *Bonfires and Bells: National Memory and the Protestant Calendar in Elizabethan and Stuart England*, revised edition (London: The History Press, 2004).

Cuming, G. J., ed., *The Durham Book: Being the First Draft of the Revision of the Book of Common Prayer in 1661* (Oxford: Oxford University Press, 1961).

Cuming, G. J., *A History of Anglican Liturgy* (London: Macmillan, 1969).

Cuming, G. J., *The Godly Order: Texts and Studies Relating to the Book of Common Prayer*, Alcuin Club (London: SPCK, 1983).

Dix, Gregory, *The Shape of the Liturgy* (London: Dacre Press, 1945).

Douglas, Mary, *Natural Symbols: Explorations in Cosmology*, 2nd edition (London: Routledge, 1996).

Duffy, Eamon, *The Stripping of the Altars: Traditional Religion in England 1400–1580* (New Haven and London: Yale University Press, 1992).

Duffy, Eamon, *Marking the Hours: English People and their Prayers* (New Haven and London: Yale University Press, 2006).

Etherington, Norman, ed., *Missions and Empire*, Oxford History of the British Empire Companion Series (Oxford: Oxford University Press, 2005).

Fincham, Kenneth, and Nicholas Tyacke, *Altars Restored: The Changing Face of English Religious Worship, 1547–c.1700* (Oxford: Oxford University Press, 2007).

Green, Ian, *The Christian's ABC: Catechisms and Catechizing in England c.1530–1740* (Oxford: Clarendon Press, 1996).

Green, Ian, *Print and Protestantism in Early Modern England* (Oxford: Oxford University Press, 2000).

Griffiths, David N., *The Bibliography of the Book of Common Prayer* (London: British Library, 2002).

Hefling, Charles, and Cynthia Shattuck, ed., *The Oxford Guide to the Book of Common Prayer: A Worldwide Survey* (New York: Oxford University Press, 2006).

Henderson, W. G., *Missale ad usum insignis Ecclesiæ eboracensis*, Surtees Society (Durham, 1874–6).

Hunt, Arnold, 'The Lord's Supper in Early Modern England', *Past and Present*, 161 (1998), 39–83.

Hunt, Arnold, *The Art of Hearing: English Preachers and their Audiences 1590–1640* (Cambridge: Cambridge University Press, 2010).

Hutton, Ronald, *The Restoration: A Political and Religious History of England and Wales 1658–1667*, revised edition (Oxford: Clarendon Press, 1993).

Hutton, Ronald, *The Rise and Fall of Merry England: The Ritual Year 1400–1700* (Oxford: Oxford University Press, 1994).

Lake, Peter, *Anglicans and Puritans?* (London: Unwin Hyman, 1988).

Le Huray, Peter, *Music and the Reformation in England 1549–1660* (Cambridge: Cambridge University Press, 1978).

Legg, J. Wickham, ed., *Cranmer's Liturgical Projects*, Henry Bradshaw Society (London, 1915).

Legg, J. Wickham, *The Sarum Missal edited from Three Early Manuscripts* (Oxford: Clarendon Press, 1916).

Lennon, Colm, *Sixteenth Century Ireland* (Dublin: Gill Books, 2005).

MacCulloch, Diarmaid, *Thomas Cranmer: A Life* (New Haven and London: Yale University Press, 1996).

MacCulloch, Diarmaid, *Tudor Church Militant: Edward VI and the Protestant Reformation* (London: Allen Lane, 1999).

MacCulloch, Diarmaid, *Reformation: Europe's House Divided, 1490–1700* (London: Allen Lane, 2003).

Major, Emma, *Madam Britannia: Women, Church, and Nation, 1712–1812* (Oxford: Oxford University Press, 2011).

Maltby, Judith, *Prayer Book and People in Elizabethan and Early Stuart England* (Cambridge: Cambridge University Press, 1998).

Marshall, Peter, *Beliefs and the Dead in Reformation England* (Oxford: Oxford University, 2002).

Milton, Anthony, *Catholic and Reformed: The Roman and Protestant Churches in English Protestant Thought* (Cambridge: Cambridge University Press, 1995).

Mirk, John, *Instructions for Parish Priests*, ed. E. Peacock, Early English Texts Society (London, 1868).

Mirk, John, *Festial*, ed. S. Powell, 2 vols, Early English Texts Society (Oxford: Oxford University Press, 2009).

Palmer, Patricia, *Language and Conquest in Early Modern Ireland* (Cambridge: Cambridge University Press, 2001).

Pfaff, Richard W., *The Liturgy in Medieval England: A History* (Cambridge: Cambridge University Press, 2009).

Procter, Francis, and W. H. Frere, *A New History of the Book of Common Prayer* (London: Macmillan, 1901).

Rappaport, Roy A., *Ritual and Religion in the Making of Humanity* (Cambridge: Cambridge University Press, 1999).

Rivers, Isabel, *Reason, Grace, and Sentiment: A Study of the Language of Religion and Ethics in England, 1660–1780*, 2 vols (Cambridge: Cambridge University Press, 2005).

Rubin, Miri, *Corpus Christi: The Eucharist in Late Medieval Culture* (Cambridge: Cambridge University Press, 1991).

Spinks, Bryan D., *Sacraments, Ceremonies and the Stuart Divines: Sacramental Theology and Liturgy in England and Scotland 1603–1662* (London: Ashgate, 2002).

Strong, Rowan, ed., *The Oxford History of Anglicanism*, 5 vols (Oxford: Oxford University Press, 2017).

Targoff, Ramie, *Common Prayer: The Language of Public Devotion in Early Modern England* (Chicago: University of Chicago Press, 2001).

Tyacke, Nicholas, *Anti-Calvinists: The Rise of English Arminianism, 1590–1640* (Oxford: Oxford University Press, 1987).

Vance, Norman, *Bible and Novel: Narrative Authority and the Death of God* (Oxford: Oxford University Press, 2013).

Wabuda, Susan, *Preaching During the English Reformation* (Cambridge: Cambridge University Press, 2002).

Walsham, Alexandra, *Providence in Early Modern England* (Oxford: Oxford University Press, 1999).

Walsham, Alexandra, *The Reformation of the Landscape: Religion, Identity, and Memory in Early Modern Britain and Ireland* (Oxford: Oxford University Press, 2012).

Wied, Hermann von, *A simple and religious consultation of us Herman Archebishop of Colone* (London: John Day, 1548).

Publisher's acknowledgements

We are grateful for permission to include the following copyright material in this book.

Extract from T. S. Eliot, *Sweeney Agonistes: Collected Poems 1909–1962* by T. S. Eliot (2002). By permission of Faber and Faber Ltd.

Extract from T. S. Eliot, *Ash Wednesday: The Poems of T.S. Eliot Volume 1* by T. S. Eliot (2015). By permission of Faber and Faber Ltd.

p.314 extract (5w) from verse 51 line 1 'inordinate wording of Common Prayer' from poem Speech! Speech! In memory of David Wright from "Broken Hierarchies" by Hill, Geoffrey edited by Haynes, Kenneth (2013), by permission of Oxford University Press.

The publisher and author have made every effort to trace and contact all copyright holders before publication. If notified, the publisher will be pleased to rectify any errors or omissions at the earliest opportunity.

Index

Index

The Book of Common Prayer

SOCIAL MEDIA
Very Short Introduction

Join our community
www.oup.com/vsi

- Join us online at the official Very Short Introductions **Facebook** page.
- Access the thoughts and musings of our authors with our online **blog**.
- Sign up for our monthly **e-newsletter** to receive information on all new titles publishing that month.
- Browse the full range of Very Short Introductions online.
- Read **extracts** from the Introductions for free.
- If you are a teacher or lecturer you can order inspection copies quickly and simply via our website.

ONLINE CATALOGUE
A Very Short Introduction

Our online catalogue is designed to make it easy to find your ideal Very Short Introduction. View the entire collection by subject area, watch author videos, read sample chapters, and download reading guides.

http://fds.oup.com/www.oup.co.uk/general/vsi/index.html

CATHOLICISM
A Very Short Introduction
Gerald O'Collins

Despite a long history of external threats and internal strife, the Roman Catholic Church and the broader reality of Catholicism remain a vast and valuable presence into the third millennium of world history. What are the origins of the Catholic Church? How has Catholicism changed and adapted to such vast and diverse cultural influences over the centuries? What great challenges does the Catholic Church now face in the twenty-first century, both within its own life and in its relation to others around the world? In this Very Short Introduction, Gerald O'Collins draws on the best current scholarship available to answer these questions and to present, in clear and accessible language, a fresh introduction to the largest and oldest institution in the world.

www.oup.com/vsi